# Know your Gucci from your Pucci!

PUCCI,
1960s

"*Anna Johnson is the Dr. Joyce Brothers of the purse world. Don't even think about buying another bag until you have inhaled ev___ ___d clutch in this bo___*"
THE NEW YORK ___

THE BOLIDE, THE BIRKIN, BUCKETS AND BAGUETTES. Moschino's smiley-face bag and Judith Leiber's whimsical minaudières. Venetian vs. Bohemian beads. The history of the handbag and the history of style. With over 900 full-color photographs, *Handbags* is an extravagance of desire, secrecy, humor, fashion, craftsmanship, art, and exuberance.

GUCCI,
1969

___KMAN PUBLISHING • NEW YORK
ISBN 0-7611-2377-6    $13.95 U.S./$21.95 CAN.
www.workman.com          PRINTED IN ITALY

I have a handle on the situation.
I have a handle on my space and contents.
My vacant hollow.
Or the items of which I house a dozen odds and ends.
I always know what I possess or what may be un-there or missing.
To study my physiognomy, one might think not much or lacking.
But closer on inspection, I am near divine and worthy of great travels.
A true companion of love and comfort, recognition, the familiar.
I have been held in such a clutch and such a love storm
by my mistress and her values.
She takes me aboard a thousand footsteps, always holding on and never once ignoring.
Mostly I am there to steady, to balance her or witness.
She sometimes shuffles through my soul in search of needy things,
like painted sticks and looking glasses of which I keep most dear.
She searches inward and there she looks inside my sacred space.
Full of painted stick and looking glasses,
I am my lady's handbag.

# CONTENTS

# Introduction

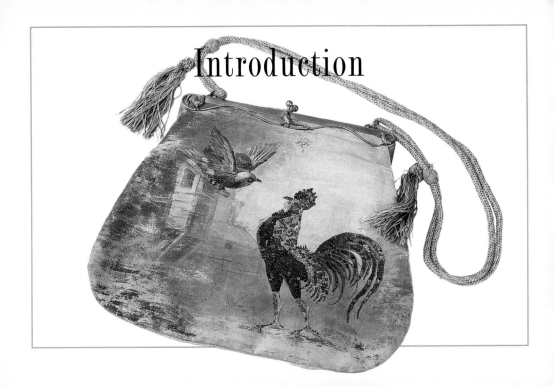

At the end of the novel *Anna Karenina,* the unhappy heroine flings herself under the wheels of an oncoming train. We know she is going to end it all when she throws her red velvet handbag onto the tracks first. A woman who is sick of her handbag, surely, is absolutely sick of living. What, save theft, could possibly compel you to release your best handbag from your grip?

*Caron of Houston, Texas, 1950s*

Marked with life, stuffed to the gills, saved for, bruised, and cherished like a child, a good bag becomes an intimate extension of the body. A second sex, but not in the way that Simone de Beauvoir imagined it. A belly for concealment. A little house for a mobile life. A portable boudoir packed with lipsticks and hair clips. A home for old letters and an archive for future generations.

*Roberta di Camerino, 1959; Previous page: French, c. 1820*

The contents of a vintage handbag form the most reliable time capsules and definitely the most honest. Opening a 1930s Cartier bag that once belonged to a showgirl, the couture collector Mark Walsh found a bottle of scent, a booklet of powdered leaves, and a pair of pink satin tap-dancing knickers (perfectly clean). The cleft between respectable exterior and intensely private interior is what gives the handbag such erotic and transgressive charge. It is perhaps a woman's last secret place.

It is easy to ridicule the handbag. The language that surrounds it is possessive and territorial: clutch, clasp, grasp, strap, and snap shut. The fiction that describes it is so

*Moschino, embroidered silk fan bag, 2000*

*American, 1940s*

often heavy handed. In "The Escape," Katherine Mansfield compares the trepidation a young husband feels about his wife as embodied by her "little bag, with its shiny, silvery jaws open." Virgins and prudes are always depicted carrying bags that are tightly sealed. Albrecht Durer represented the purity of Mary by the closed purse of Joachim. Psychiatrists have always held the bag in suspicion, imagining it to be a "vagina dentata"—the only place a man's hands are unwelcome.

Artists and writers have had their fun with the purse as well. Surrealists sliced them up for collages and sculptures. In Samuel Beckett's play *Happy Days,* a woman's whole life is (quite literally) contained within her bag; for Winnie, who's buried up to her armpits in a mound of dirt, her handbag is her past and her only present—the sole prop to get her through the day. Diana Vreeland railed against the dangling accessory, urging women to "Ban the bag!" and patch their pants and coats instead with gigantic pockets. Germaine Greer growled at the pocketbook, complaining that it was the symbolic vessel of woman's servile role. But is it really? Some of the most potent women of the 20th century cut a swath through a man's world with this most feminine of objects. Fleet Street feared the parliamentary power of Margaret Thatcher to the extent that a new term for bullying and political coercion was added to the *Oxford English Dictionary:* handbagging. Thatcher never went anywhere without the chunky purse she called her "trusty companion."

*Bohemian, 1920s*

More than just political power, a great bag (carried by a great lady) has class. Grace Kelly is the most famous and still the most elegant example of this. After she was featured on the front of *Life*

*Grace Kelly— her bag moment*

magazine in 1956 using an Hermès bag to shield her pregnant belly from photographers, her demure gesture launched a collective fantasy: that a bag could make you a diplomat, a diva, and a survivor. That a bag could transform your existence from commoner to princess. A smart bag promises so much. The idea of owning one classic bag is sensibly old fashioned. An heirloom bag that will hold together longer than your face seems a wise investment. Granny would approve.

*American, 1960s*

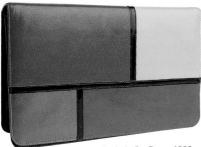

*Jack de La Rose, 1980s*

Yet unlike our grandmothers, very few women today are content to own just one good bag.

No, no, *no!* Instead, we hanker for classic bags *and* the "It" bag of the season *and* work bags *and* a sexy little bag for evening. We need a big mother-ship tote for the office and a satellite (or dinghy) bag for short forays beyond, we need a weekend bag, a witty bag for a cellphone, and a basket bag for the first day of spring. When Coco Chanel described luxury as "the necessity where necessity ends," she defined the irrational passion for the handbag so well. Of course we could get through life with a big set of pockets and a small drawstring pouch for evening, as they did in the 18th century. Certainly we could subsist with a carpet bag for travel and a leather purse for shopping

*Chanel, 2002*

*American, 1940s*

like a Victorian lady. Most of our paperwork could fit into a masculine briefcase or a sensible backpack, but that isn't the point.

The ideal handbag, like a beautiful shoe, has never really been about necessity. It is the stuff of dreams, desire, and deliverance from the banal. It is that house in the country we can't afford embodied in Italian straw, it is a first kiss in cherry-red velvet, a movie star flash of rhinestones or a crush of glossy patent leather from Paris, France. A portable fashion object unperturbed by the changes of the body or the heavy hand of age, the bag is infinitely optimistic. We carry it, and it transports us into the lives we wish we were living.

## HOW THE BAG WAS BORN

The very first bag was probably a fistful of skins tied to a bit of stick, a provisional container for food and flint. From these simple beginnings, the bag has blossomed into every form, color, and material imaginable. The earliest bag in this book, a pouch from 5th-century Scythia, is now a little worse for wear. Like so many bags of ancient times, it is a pouch that was worn dangled from the waist. From the Coliseum to the Christian Crusades, the drawstring purse was

*Scythian pouch,*
*5th century*

the bag most consistently used by both men and women. The development of a metal frame enlarged the size of the bag and gave it a little more structure, but it was still worn around the waist and hips, especially fashionable on the ornate girdles women wore from the 13th to the 15th century. Through the Middle Ages, bags enjoyed androgyny, set apart only by minor variations of ornament and contents peculiar to each sex.

The cult of the tiny, embellished bag for the lady of style started with the almoner, a showy coin purse designed to draw attention to public display of largesse. From the

*German almoner,*
*15th century*

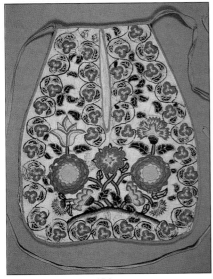

*Pear-shaped pocket, 17th century;*
*Right: Ottoman reticule, 1810*

beginning, small bags inferred class. Big bulky shoulder bags or pouches worn astride the body implied a hard day's work and were for peasants only. As skirts grew voluminous in the 16th century, women secreted their valuables in their folds, into muffs, and even up their sleeves, but by the 17th century a better solution was found. Pretty pear-shaped pockets were worn tied to each hip beneath hooped petticoats. A woman's pocket was not sewn into her dress, whereas the sewn-in pockets that 17th-century men came to depend on did away with the need for a hanging purse or a large fancy wallet. And this is where the story of the bag divides the sexes.

The separate pockets that women now wore tied around their waists gave them a taste for toting their personal effects about, a liberty few would part with. When the sheer empire-line dress fashion was introduced in Paris in 1790, it gave birth to the handbag. The reticule was fashion's first act of logic: to take the pocket, put it on a string, and carry it in the hand. The first such external pocket bags were called reticules after the Latin reticulum. Freshly associated with knickers and petticoats, the bags were mocked by the French press and renamed "ridicules."

*Above right:*
*French, 18th century*

By 1805 the flack over ladies wearing underwear as outerwear had settled down, and not a woman alive would leave the house without her bag. Now strictly a feminine accessory, bags were lost to men, who were stuck forevermore with their hands in their pockets. Much humor surrounded the birth of this great divide; as one wag quipped in the British *Imperial Weekly Gazette,* "While men have their hands in their pockets so grand, ladies have pockets to wear in their hand."

The first real leather handbag came a little later, when a sturdy tote with handles was needed for travel. Based

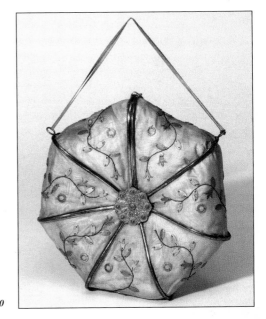

*Turkish, 1810*

on luggage, the handbag of the 1860s was a miniature suitcase complete with lock, key, and a ticket compartment within. Unlike a flimsy mesh reticule or a decorative coin purse sealed by a string, this bag snapped shut, and for the first time women could carry their things with some degree of privacy. Men, who had long carried a lady's fan or her money, were supplanted by increasingly practical, brilliantly structured bags, and they have been mystified and excluded by the handbag ever since. Who needed to be dependent on a husband when Elsa Schiaparelli's Lanterne

*German lady's travel bag, 1860s*

handbag (of 1938) could hold cigarettes, makeup, keys, money, and an electric light?

You can't discuss the history of the handbag without also discussing female independence, for how a woman carried her chattel relates closely to how she carried herself. In the 14th century a lady paraded her worldly goods from a chain on her hip. In the 21st century her wealth may be implied by the opulence of her bag but it is never truly revealed. The power of the handbag (and of a woman) dwells in solidity, secrecy, and graceful self-containment.

*Comtesse, 1990*

# one

# Class Acts: Elegant Icons

The idea of an important bag, a bag that announces both status and substance, began in the 19th century but was perfected in the 20th. The classic bag began with the horse and the steamship. Louis Vuitton made traveling trunks for Napoleon III, and Hermès were saddlers to the aristocracy. Prada and Gucci both made quality baggage, and Fendi sold luxury leather goods and furs. The success of these houses depended on their adaptability to the modern age and ingenious inventions brought on by necessity. What appears today to be classically conservative was radical in its time. Louis Vuitton had logos hand painted on his canvas travel trunks in 1896

*Fendi travel bags, 1980s;*
*Previous page: Christian Dior, 2000*

*Hermès, 1999*

to defy the counterfeiters. Emile-Maurice Hermès had the wit to transform feed bags and saddlebags into elegant handbag shapes and turned the Canadian army cargo zipper into the first truly modern fashion fastening, bringing it back to Paris in 1923. After the war, when leather supplies were scarce, Gucci turned to cotton canvas and bamboo handles. Chanel whipped the weighted gilt chains out of the hems of her suits and fashioned them into the shoulder straps of her famous quilted 2/1955 bag.

Such rich history is what creates the pedigree and enigmatic lure of a classic handbag, and many contemporary designers attempt to mine that history, creating hybrid bags that greedily snatch at saddle stitching, gold hardware, monogram prints, and whatever else it takes to make an "It" bag. But the "It" bag is not necessarily

*Green Kelly bag, 1991, and Red Birkin, 1984*

an overnight classic. Classics, like a strong vintage, take time. Before the era of designer think tanks, major advertising campaigns, and calculated attempts to win Anna Wintour's good graces, the great houses relied on standard designs that changed very little over the years.

Hermès created the four classic handbag shapes of the 20th century by making the leap from the horse to the automobile. Their most famous bag, called the Haut à Courroies because

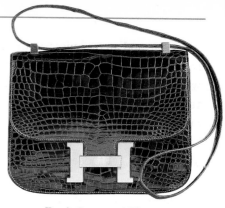

*Hermès Constance, 1969*

of its tall shape and long straps, was created in 1892 to hold a saddle. In 1930 the bag was adapted for travel, and became madly famous in 1956 when Princess Grace Kelly posed with hers on the cover of *Life* magazine. In 1923 the Bolide bag was the first in history to feature a zipper; Emile-Maurice designed it for his wife as a driving bag. The Plume, designed in 1930, was based on a horse blanket bag but applied in a much more modern way: practical and pliable, this was the first shape that could double as a day bag and an overnighter. In 1958 a bucketlike feed bag was made elegant with a scooped gusset and skinny strap and was christened the Trim. Jacqueline Onassis wore the bag around Capri in the late '60s, making it a resort standard. The shapes of these four bags seem outrageously simple: an elongated triangle, an elliptical square, a soft little box shaped like a caramel, and a simple hobo. Yet these are the four forms that most classic bags are based on today.

*Louis Vuitton*
*Noe, 2001*

Louis Vuitton's marvelous bucket-shaped shoulder bag was designed to carry five bottles of champagne. The Noe (born in 1932) sprang up from a design imagination fixated on travel. The house of Vuitton began with a journey. Fourteen-year-old Louis Vuitton took a year-long walk to Paris in 1836 to find his fortune. Traveling rough made an impact on the rural Frenchman. In a swift

*Chanel, 1953*

ascension from official luggage packer for Empress Eugenie, Vuitton set his carpentry skills to creating the most luxurious steamer trunks in Europe. Inventing both the monogram logo and the first sturdy travel canvas, Vuitton applied both to a unique bag aesthetic devoted to streamlined form. The steamer bag of 1901 and the Keep-all, designed in 1924, formed the blueprint for almost all totes, career bags, and travel bags to follow. Tall, with a front flap and tidy belt, the steamer shares its long lines and masculine charm with the later Hermès Birkin bag. Its tiny handle was designed to hang on the back of a cabin door. Neatly horizontal, we look at the Keep-all today as a classic tennis bag or duffel. Both bags seem almost perplexingly simple, yet in the context of the ruffled petticoats, hats, and gloves of their day, they were starkly modern.

*Chanel, 1955*

Not all classics have such an ancient history; many had to be reinvented before they found their following. Chanel's square quilted bag with a chain strap was released in February 1955 and, like her signature perfume, Chanel No. 5, bluntly named after the number of its birth date: 2/1955. Discreet and unmonogrammed (the initials were sewn on the inside), the bag worked well with the neat jersey suits that marked Chanel's comeback and kept selling after her death in 1971. But the bag did not become a cult classic until Chanel's new designer Karl Lagerfeld jazzed it up in the '80s. Lagerfeld fattened the chain, slapped a massive interlocking-Cs logo on the front, and worked it in all sizes, from a cigarette case to a tote. The Chanel bag was a classic set to disco, eclipsing the Kelly as *the* status

*Chanel, 2001*

bag of the '80s. Its success challenged many old houses to revive their best iconic features and fine-tune them into handbags, especially after overlicensing in the '70s had diluted their names by spreading logos far and wide. The return to classic style in the late '80s and early '90s signaled serious recovery of both prestige and revenue for the big design houses.

*Prada, 1992*

Miuccia Prada took the somewhat fusty old-world elegance of her grandfather's Milanese leather house and used the name, rather than the house style, to forge her first cult bag. Her radical departure into luxury sportswear style inverted the status system. By making the bag simple (a black, ripstop nylon backpack) and the logo subtle but luxe, she gave the designer logo renewed street credibility. Suddenly the status bag could look young and hip again. Her collections used classic, deliberately masculine shapes (the lunch box, the medicine bag) in flighty evening fabrics: silk, velvet, satin. Clever designers create modern classics by subverting existing traditions or simply enriching them. The house of Dior reentered the stratosphere of luxury bags with the Lady Dior. A cocktail of decorative overstitching and a cluster of logo letters dangled from the handle like a charm bracelet, giving the Lady Dior the look of precious bibelot. When Madame Chirac presented the bag to Lady Diana in 1995 during Diana's visit to Paris, she proceeded to parade it across the world, reviving the legend of the princess and the handbag.

When Tom Ford came on board as creative director of Gucci in 1992 he retained a few choice elements of early Gucci—the classic bamboo handle, the glossy silver insignia, and

*Lady Dior, 2001*

*Fendi
Selleria,
2002*

the bold striped canvas—and made us all forget the muddy brown blur of the '70s logo bag. At Fendi the Selleria line revived the saddler techniques and old-fashioned hexagonal forms of the house's travel bags from the '20s. Made by hand from a pebbly naturally treated cowhide (the *cuoio fiore*), finished with beautifully simple saddle stitches, and released in a limited edition each season (indicated by a serial number embossed on a silver plaque inside each bag), these bags soon attracted cultish waiting lists. Waiting lists add a potent charge to a bag's cachet, conveying the tension between modern appetites and ancient production methods.

Quality creates demand; rarity doubles it. Combining scarcity, tradition, and ancient technique, the hallmarks of a classic handbag are both conservative and escapist. It is a style that runs like a vein of gold through the

*Louis Vuitton
Cluny, 1990s*

daydreams of the passionate window-shopper. Ultimately these quiet-looking bags provoke demonic levels of desire. The rationale for spending seven hundred to seven thousand dollars on a mere handbag can't be rational: aside from the sober investment in quality, history, and elegance, we are drawn to something far more provocative than that. Luxury is aggression dressed as fashion, the crest that divides you from the crowd and makes your power explicit.

Magic, mystery, and money are all wrapped up in the myth of a classic handbag. We wear them to look more powerful, composed, or posh than we really are. Designers play on such aspirations, aware that women are searching for their personal motto and fictional selves. As a feminine trophy for succeeding in a man's world or a fragment of a life that is perpetually beyond your reach, the classic bag remains a stubborn, bewitching fixture. Call it handbag utopia.

*Ferragamo, 1991*

CELEBRITIES MAKE
HANDBAG HEADLINES.
When Grace Kelly
carried the Hermès
Haut à Courroies bag,
a cult sprang up around
the bag, and never went
away. Ingrid Bergman
and Marlene Dietrich
had carried the same bag,
but to much less acclaim.

HERMÈS, 2001

THE HEIR OF HERMÈS, Jean-Louis Dumas, saw the humor in the beloved Kelly. He transformed the bag into a doll and called it "Quelle Idole" in a limited edition designed to celebrate the millennium.

HERMÈS, 2000

FOUR PARENTS, ENDLESS OFFSPRING. That's the best way to describe the impact of the most influential bags of the 20th century. Soft and tapered, the Bolide bag designed by Hermès in 1923 was the first bag in the world to use a zipper. Introduced a decade later, the Plume was originally designed to carry a horse blanket.

LOUIS VUITTON NOE BAG, 1932

HERMÈS BOLIDE, 1923

Its simple travel shape spearheaded the minimal modernist handbag. The Trim, designed in 1958, became a jet-set symbol after Jackie O. sported hers in Capri; few know that this classic was based on a horse feed bag. The Noe bag was designed to hold five bottles of champagne. It epitomized Louis Vuitton's philosophy of travel: elegance can and will be taken on the road.

HERMÈS PLUME, 1933

HERMÈS LE TRIM, 1958

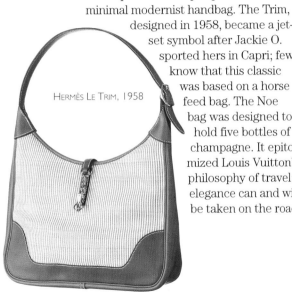

HORSE AND HOUND are never far away from the equestrian aesthetics of a status bag. The leaping greyhound of Trussardi's logo adopts racing colors in this extravagant tote.

TRUSSARDI, 2001

TURNING THE HOUSE LOGO into stirrups was John Galliano's witty vision for the modern saddle bag.

CHRISTIAN DIOR, 2001

NECESSITY IS THE MOTHER
of inventive style.
Leather shortages after
World War II forced
Aldo Gucci to put cane
handles on his bags.

GUCCI, C. 1969–75

Miniature cane bags provide a cute little novelty and coin purse in one.

JILL STUART, 1990

Big, black, and bold as brass, the Chanel bag was the most coveted status symbol of the 1980s. Exploded to the size of a shoulder tote with the famous monogram and gilt shoulder chain writ large, Karl Lagerfeld's creation was the ultimate power-bitch statement: a professional attaché case and gloriously loud handbag in one.

CHANEL, 1980s

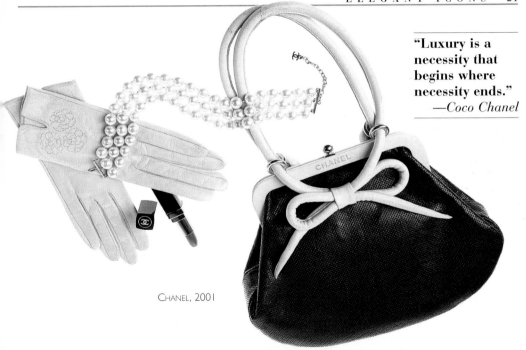

"Luxury is a
necessity that
begins where
necessity ends."
—*Coco Chanel*

CHANEL, 2001

Hot on the heels of the Chanel bag revival, black and gold came to rule '80s status dressing with quilted, plaited, and stitched leathers offset by whimsical hardware.

Bottega Veneta, 1980s

GUCCI PASTA CLASP BAG,
LATE 1980s

LIGHTENING UP to stay current, Chanel indulges a taste for novelty. The limited-edition "shopping bag" of hard plastic and gold-studded mesh is just the thing for the *supermarché*.

CHANEL SHOPPER, 1997

**"Fashion is made to become unfashionable."**
*—Coco Chanel*

CHANEL JACKET BAG,
2002

STREAMLINED FOR OCEAN LINERS, the first Louis Vuitton steamer bag is said to have been inspired by the simple proportions of a Mexican postal bag. Designed to hang on the hook of a steamship cabin door, this bag is a precursor to the modern backpack.

LOUIS VUITTON STEAMER, 1901

LOUIS VUITTON monogram canvas is waterproof. So much so that '60s millionaire Gunther Sachs claimed to have tossed his luggage out of a helicopter near Saint-Tropez and pushed it through the water to Brigitte Bardot's feet, and that it arrived with all contents perfectly intact. The bags impressed. She married him.

LOUIS VUITTON, 2000

THE RAREST BIRD in the handbag world dwells on the face of a Baguette hand woven from ostrich and peacock feathers with eighteen-karat gold threads ornamenting its beak. This limited-edition luxury bag was cut from silk created on Renaissance looms.

FENDI BAGUETTE, 2001

A BITE-SIZED PLEASURE, the Croissant bag was the offspring of the Baguette and was all the more precious for its sheer lack of practicality. Shaped like a crescent moon and just big enough for a cell phone and a fortune cookie, the bag was proposed as a little luxury pouch for life's essentials, to be carried in the belly of a bigger bag.

FENDI CROISSANT, 2000

# SILVIA VENTURINI FENDI: EMPRESS OF STYLE

The Fendi flagship store in Rome is laid out like an exotic bazaar, with long low tables crowded with bags that look like sugar-dusted cakes, soft lighting, and a dizzying selection of merchandise. Unlike in the starchier luxury houses, very little is behind glass, and you want to caress and handle it all. It must have been that way for Silvia Venturini Fendi as a child visiting her aunts' opulent palazzos and watching "Uncle Karl" Lagerfeld tint mink coats violet and apricot pink at the atelier. Rich heritage has produced a style the press has dubbed "Maximalist"; for Fendi it is a matter of blood. "I carry within myself a very strong visual historic and emotional memory which is tied to Fendi's history and to my personal life," she says.

The Fendi Baguette was not baked overnight. It was a bag born of a Roman matriarch, and three generations of

*Selleria Baguette, 2002*

*First Fendi store, Rome*

women devoted to style. The latest of the line, Silvia Venturini Fendi had an opulent and eccentric heritage to draw on. Edoardo and Adele Fendi opened a leather and fur workshop on the Via del Plebiscito in Rome in 1925. The first bags they sold were hand stitched and pliable. Adele gave birth to five daughters, and as babies they slept in the handbag drawer at the shop. The proximity to luxury and leather rubbed off. Paola, Anna, Franca, Carla, and Alda Fendi all joined the company after World War II and applied their jet-set style to an essentially conservative firm. In 1965 they hired Karl Lagerfeld, who brought panache to the house and developed a radical approach to fur and a super-sophisticated brand of ready-to-wear. Seventies and '80s Fendi bags dripped with slick caramel and chocolate stripes, but by the '90s it was time for change. Prada had grooved up their bag and logo for a new generation, and the trends of

*Fendi, 1992*

grunge and vintage romanticism were challenging the grand old houses to concoct a different vision for the handbag.

When she started work at the atelier as design coordinator in 1992, Silvia Venturini Fendi saw "plastic, normal, plain, ugly things." She sought to remedy the obvious disparity between the outrageous furs, the beautiful clothes, and the rather pedestrian handbags. Influenced by eastern textiles, eccentric ornament, and neo-70s hippie chic, Fendi introduced richer colors and wilder fabrics. Her timing was perfect. The Baguette arrived at a moment

*Silvia Venturini Fendi*

### A bevy of Baguettes, 1999–2002

*Lisio velvet and silk embroidery*

*Leather and straw*

*Raffia, silk, and straw*

*Enamel, crystals, and screen-printed leather*

when women wanted to be peacocks instead of black sheep. Season after season, the prevailing trend in bags had been minimal and pragmatic; boxy Kate Spade totes and sensible black nylon Prada backpacks had dominated fashion. In March 1997 the Baguette provided a sumptuous alternative. Ornamented with a bold interlocking logo, two silver buckles, and an abbreviated strap, it was released in a glamorous array of colors and luxe materials. Its diminutive scale, soft body, and short little strap made it a discreet luxury, tucked under the arm like a stealthy little jewel. Seasonal changes to the bag and limited numbers of each collection also managed to keep baguettes in demand. Described by British fashion writer Marion Hume as "beanie babies for grown-ups," the bags flipped from denim to velvet to paillette sequins every six

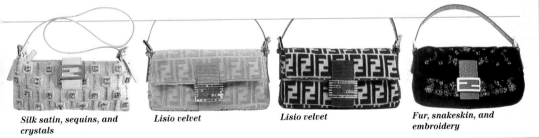

*Silk satin, sequins, and crystals*     *Lisio velvet*     *Lisio velvet*     *Fur, snakeskin, and embroidery*

months. Sophia Loren compared her penchant for collecting them to a drug addiction.

After creating such a blockbuster, the pressure on Fendi to provide an encore was intense. Quickly after came the Croissant, a bag no bigger than a slice of grapefruit, and a revivial of the Selleria line, handstitched *cuoio* leather bags inspired by the travel goods created back in the '20s. The earthy, stripped-back feeling of a Selleria medicine bag, with its slightly pebbled skin and rough-hewn heavy stitching is not at all giddy or faddish. It looks, in fact, almost exactly like the bag Fendi's grandfather would have carried—done in lipstick red.

*Selleria bag, 2001*

Going back to go forward seemed a natural step to the third-generation designer, who had grown up with the master of unsentimental change, Karl Lagerfeld, as a mentor. Each of her collections is marked by stark contrasts. "When I design," she says, "I think of a Fendi bag as a particular object—right for a particular moment. I obsess about the materials of the bag to the point of exhaustion. To make an object that is singular and unique takes great concentration and every detail is precise and studied." So a collection of fragile feminine beaded bags is followed by futuristic op-art shoulder totes, hand-loomed silk velvets sit alongside positively macho hand-beaten bronze "Ostrik" bags and tooled-leather models that look like they were carved by a drunken Fauvist.

Uniting it all is a sense of touch, artisanal details like embroidery and hand carving that lend a rustic warmth to such hard-core glamour. Citing "creativity, research, courage, and determination" as the secrets of her success, the third woman in the Fendi matriarchal line sounds less like a handbag designer and more like a Roman senator. And why not? Her empire is built on baroque aesthetics, bugle beads, bestsellers, and brave choices.

*Ostrik bag, 2002*

*Spoon bag, 2001*

UNTIL THE '80s the Louis
Vuitton logo was sacrosanct.
Little by little, the house
branched out. Marc Jacobs
discovered that disrupting
the logo gave it the most
cachet. In 2000 he had pop
artist Stephen Sprouse
spray a graffiti version
of the name across the
canvas, and the collector's
item became the "It" bag
of the season.

LOUIS VUITTON, 2000

VEII PUCELLE, 2001

HONEY AND BEIGE are the handbag equivalent of a year-round tan. They're high-maintenance colors, declaring utter detachment from utility. The design for Jeffrey Sperber's VEII Pucelle bag was based on upscale French luggage of the 1940s. Moschino's notion of practical luxury is a duffel with diamond buckles.

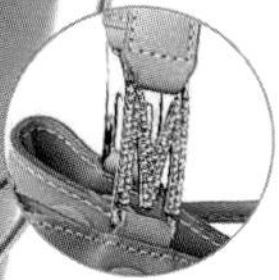

MOSCHINO, 2001

Salvatore Ferragamo made disparate materials dance—silk and cork, canvas and ribbon, leather and solid gold. In homage to that eccentric spirit, this bag matches straps of gold medallions and grosgrain ribbon with a hula skirt of cut raffia.

Ferragamo, 1997

"There is no limit to beauty,
no saturation point in design."
—*Salvatore Ferragamo*

FERRAGAMO, CAST ALUMINUM, 1996

BORN AS BESPOKE, the lineage
of the classic handbag is
surprisingly consistent.
Hermès catalogue pages
from the '20s are
as discreet and
streamlined as
contemporary
collections,
with a charac-
teristic
emphasis
on wealth,
leisure and
*le mode sportif.*

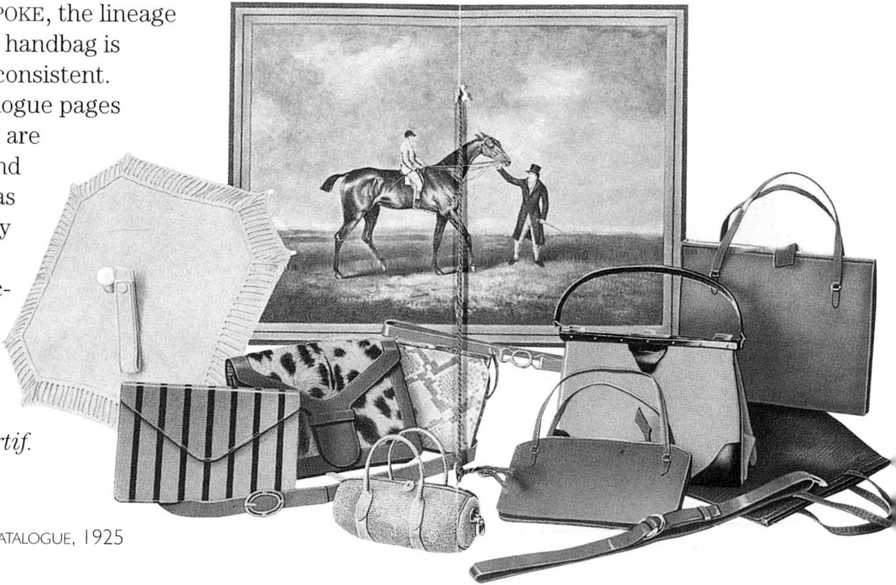

HERMÈS CATALOGUE, 1925

HAGGLED FOR ON *SEX AND THE CITY,* back ordered for up to eighteen months, and the price of two first-class tickets to Gstaad, the Hermès Birkin bag was originally designed for bohemian actress Jane Birkin, who was known to carry her in-flight reading in a straw basket.

HERMÈS, 2001

L<small>AUNCHED IN</small> S<small>EPTEMBER</small> 1995, the Lady Dior bag was presented to Lady Diana at the Grand Palais in Paris. This was the second Dior bag to be made famous by a controversial royal. Wallis Simpson, the duchess of Windsor, was presented with a smart little Dior bag with a carved amber handle in 1950.

C<small>HRISTIAN</small> D<small>IOR</small>, L<small>ADY</small> D<small>IOR</small>, 1995

JOHN GALLIANO leads the classic Dior houndstooth in a tribal war dance complete with lap-lap fringing and faux ivory handles.

CHRISTIAN DIOR, 1999

THE COUTURE BAG didn't always match the frock and shoe. Christian Dior rarely paraded the bag with the dress. It was not until the '90s that the handbag became an integral part of the Dior couture collection. This idea is expressed spectacularly by John Galliano's Trailer bag.

CHRISTIAN DIOR, 2001

SOMETHING OLD, something new, something borrowed, something freaky. Mad riffs on classic themes permit John Galliano to take liberties with Dior's New Look. Here a weekend bag looks like a very plump set of hips wearing the tailored, lightly padded suit that changed the shape of fashion in 1946.

CHRISTIAN DIOR, 2001

LOGO MANIA REACHED saturation point in the '70s and again in the '90s when the bag was eaten alive by its own monogram.

MOSCHINO, 2000

TINSELTOWN OF HOLLYWOOD ridiculed the trend by replacing the status name with something more profane, and irreverent.

TINSELTOWN CANVAS AND VINYL BAG, 1971

"I would shed tears the day
no one copied me."
—*Coco Chanel*

CHANEL PATENT LEATHER BEACH BAG
AND MATCHING PURSE, 2001

SUMMER IN SARDINIA?
Solve the problem
of a bag that goes
from café society to
flirting surfside with
detachable inserts in silk
and terry cloth.

FERRAGAMO, 1995

GLOSSY PATENT LEATHER in babydoll colors was a radical reinterpretation of the Vuitton logo, and the Vernis bag by Marc Jacobs brought the label to a younger, less formal generation.

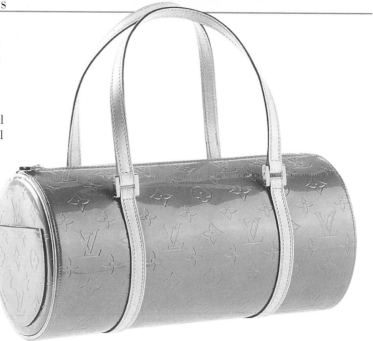

LOUIS VUITTON VERNIS, 1998–99

A CULT HAS SPRUNG up around the Selleria series, the handmade saddle-stitched bags that are released in limited editions each season. They come with a serial number embossed on a silver plaque, a bit like a medal for collectors.

FENDI SELLERIA DOCTOR'S BAG, 2001

GUCCI BAGS,
MID-1950S
TO MID-1970S

1957

1964

THE DEMAND FOR DISCREET little day bags in the early '60s generated designs that stressed delicate detail— elegant straps, geometric hardware, and the signature striped canvas teamed subtly with suede.

1975

1978

"If a bag is attractive, it
makes you feel good by
default. It's all about
proportion, shape, line,
finish, fabric, balance.
If all of that is pleasing
it will sell. More than
that it's like you've gotta
have it or you'll die."
—*Tom Ford,
creative director, Gucci*

GUCCI, 2002

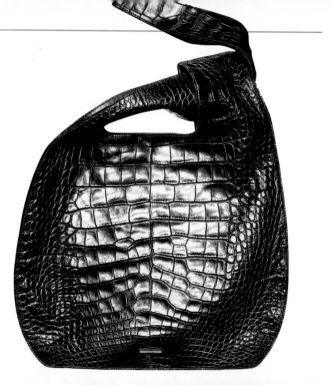

BLACK IS the new black at Gucci.

GUCCI, 2002

IT TAKES TWO ALLIGATORS to make a Kelly bag. The best of the exotic skin is culled from the jowls and the belly of the beast. The belly is used for the body of the bag, and the neck skin, supple from all that snapping, becomes the sides.

HERMÈS ALLIGATOR KELLY BAG, 1956

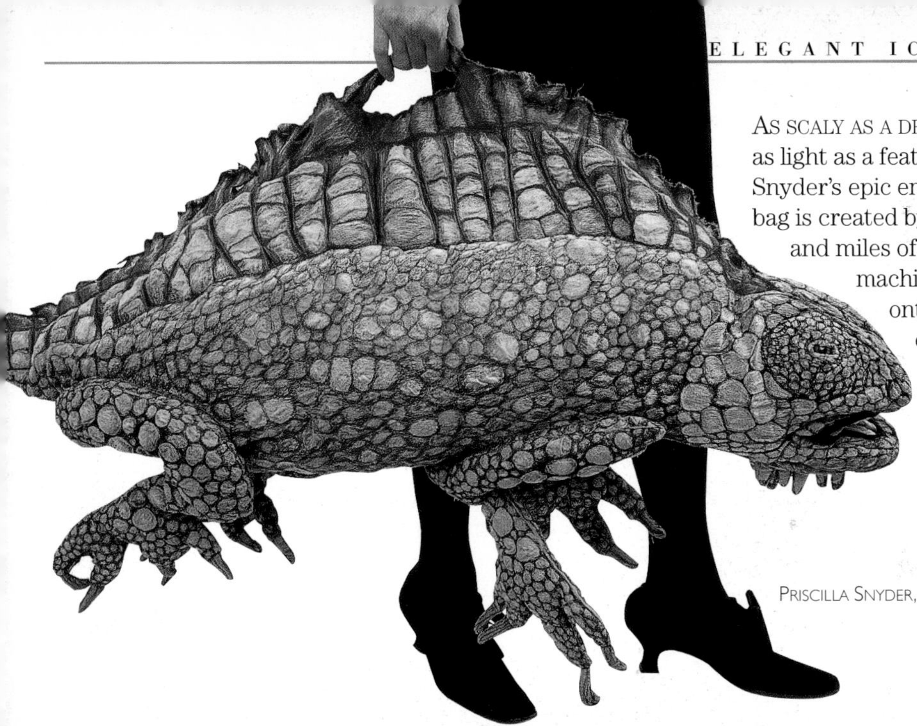

AS SCALY AS A DRAGON and as light as a feather, Priscilla Snyder's epic embroidered bag is created by sewing miles and miles of multicolored machine stitches onto a sturdy cotton canvas.

PRISCILLA SNYDER, 1997

# How a Kelly Bag is Made

I magining an Hermès Kelly bag in pieces is like imagining Grace Kelly in rollers. Both icons of 20th-century style live in the mind perfectly put together, with nothing unfinished or deconstructed about them. Strangely smooth and solid for a humble creation of skin and thread, the Kelly bag admits few secrets.

Eighteen hours with one craftsman is how such solidity is attained. Like all Hermès handbags, the Kelly is made

*Structured, or hard Kelly bag, 1956*

by a single craftsman from the first stitch to the last. The skins (selected according to personal customer order) arrive hand-cut in pieces. Laid out flat, the body of the bag looks like a mini-dress with a slightly broad belly, the notches of

*Soft Kelly bag, 1956*

the distinctive front flap resembling arm holes. The lining, which is always of goat skin, is the first part to be sewn. The base of the bag is then handstitched to the front and the back with waxed linen thread. Hermès artisans use a double saddle stitch that pierces the leather on both sides. Each stitch is painstakingly adjusted to the individual grain and density of the leather. Before every stitch, a tiny hole must be made in the leather with a pointed instrument called an awl. The stitch size dictates the size of the awl, and meticulous care is taken with every perforation.

The next step is the creation of the handle. That lovely sculptured arc is shaped by hand using a special knife and five individual pieces of leather. The distinct, beveled edges of the layers of leather are smoothed away with sandpaper and then dyed to match the bag as closely as possible. Hot wax seals this part of the bag, protecting

*Hermès's classic, double saddle stitch*

*It takes two legs and two steady hands to be a human sewing machine.*

*The signature locking belt hardware.*

it from moisture. Then the front flap is stitched, again by hand, to the body of the bag. The handles are glued and stitched to the bag. The clasp and the four little square feet of the base are hand-riveted to the exterior skin. Next, the four distinctive holes are punctured to admit the bag's famous locking belt hardware.

One honored tenet at Hermès is to make the inside of the bag as impeccable as the exterior. Poke inside a soft Kelly bag and you will feel the smooth line of the leather's edge forming a gentle mounded curve. That's because the bag's seams involve the same painstaking process as the handle—smoothing the leather, dying, and then waxing it. The most surprising finishing touch of this eighteen-hour process is a gentle ironing of the bag. Getting the crinkles out of calfskin is the penultimate step to perfection. The last is a christening with the famous "Hermès Paris" name stamped in gold on each offspring.

*Left: Kelly, 2001;*
*Right: Silk scarf Kelly,*
*early '90s*

THE ARCHIVES OF THE GREAT HOUSES breed fresh litters of handbags each season. When the Roman design duo Pierpaolo Piccioli and Maria Grazia Chiuri moved from Fendi to Valentino Garavani, they drew inspiration from the atelier's swinging '60s style.

VALENTINO GARAVANI, 2001

HANDBAG STYLE is a matter of perpetual cross-pollination. Blink and you miss the differences between this late '60s Gucci and the modern Valentino it so closely resembles.

GUCCI, 1969

WHAT'S YOUR PURSE-ONALITY?
Parisian artist Natalie Lecroc reads
handbags the way a medium reads
tea leaves, then paints a playful
"portrait." "It's not so much the
bag itself or the individual things
in it," says Lecroc, "but everything
together that forms the signature
of personality"—the interior life
of the sitter. Here, the contents of
Lyn Revson's *sac* are as regal as
Marie Antoinette's toilette—with
solid gold hairbrush, compact,
and pill box. The sitter's one
concession to real life? Three
candies in plastic wrappers.

NATALIE LECROC, 2002

> **"My work has consisted of cutting off what others added."**
>
> —*Coco Chanel*

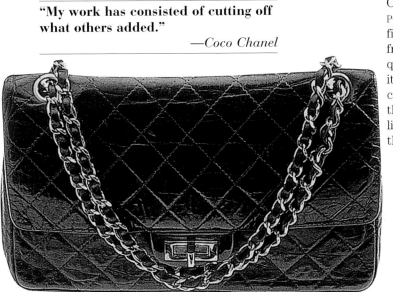

CHANEL LOVED POCKETS, and her first handbags grew from there. Square, quilted, and wearing its monogram discreetly on the inside, this chic *pratique* little gem was called the 2/1955.

CHANEL, 1955

PUNKY BUCKLES and new-wave color give staid elegance a welcome jolt.

FENDI, 2001

BOTTEGA VENETA, 2001

THE MORE ECCENTRIC
modern classics
compress different
eras into one design.
A neo-Edwardian
doctor's bag with
scalloped leather
ruffles is equal parts
Oscar Wilde and
Doctor Seuss.

LAMBERTSON TRUEX, 2001

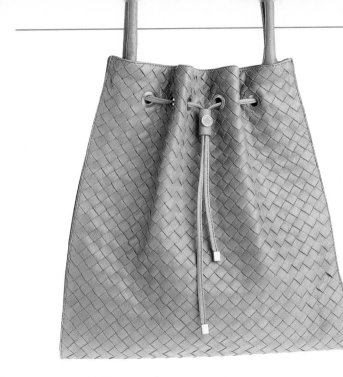

"INTERCIATTO" is the name of the woven leather used by Bottega Veneta. Supple and buttery soft, it mellows even more with age.

BOTTEGA VENETA, 2001

PLAITED LEATHER is the signature of French designer Stephane Kélian. Exaggerating the house style, this bag explodes the weave to a larger, louder scale.

STEPHANE KÉLIAN, 2001

# two

# Night Creatures: The Evening Bag

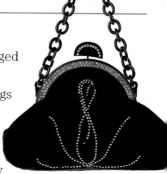

*Revivals, 1999*

**B**e a caterpillar by day and a butterfly by night, urged Coco Chanel, and how the evening bag listened. Designed to beguile and inspire deepest envy, bags for night have always had snob and sex appeal. This is the bag created solely for glamour, untethered by practical concerns.

Born as a coin purse hung loosely from a golden girdle, the first evening bags of the 13th and 14th centuries were spliced together from the embroidered remnants of wall hangings and ecclesiastical vestments. The medieval lady had no pockets, so her almoner (a coin purse for alms) was on permanent display.

This smug little bag, worn with self-conscious piety,

*Italian gaming bag, 18th century;*
*Previous page: Anthony Luciano, 2001*

set the tone for all evening bags to follow, transcending the everyday, putting on airs, or just plain showing off. Elizabethans wore evening purses elaborately crocheted into the shapes of frogs, walnuts, or clusters of grapes. Today Oscar hopefuls hit the red carpet cradling a Judith Leiber polar bear or ladybug with exactly the same intention: evening bags are showstoppers.

Bags for night allowed women autonomy over their pleasures and a certain worldly wit. Gaming bags for both men and women of the 17th century were festooned with allegorical symbols and pithy sayings pertaining to thrift, but were designed with generous bottoms for a night's winnings. As the demands of social coquetry became more complex, involving fans, perfumes, and calling cards, the need for elegant receptacles

*English,*
*16th century*

*Italian, 1900–10*

became more pressing. When little more than minute wrist bags were available to 18th-century ladies, clever belles adapted large silk "knotting" bags to carry what they needed at night. The lacy "work bag'" was the rococo equivalent of underwear as outerwear—a big crocheted and beribboned sack whipped straight out of the boudoir and worn nonchalantly over one arm. To get away with brandishing such an intimate item at the opera, a woman might display a little handwork to justify the bulk. The night tote à la mode did not last long. The 18th-century woman was probably the last in history to carry an evening bag with a generous belly. Since then they have been shrinking. Worn barely-there, like the sandal, the tiny evening bag

*Renard Paris, Renaissance revival, 1915*

advertises a modest if painfully contrived femininity. It displays the inverse snobbery of not how much one can carry, but how little. Anything more than a teacup-sized reticule implied a lack of a servant two centuries ago, the lack of a male escort one century ago, and the lack of a credit card in this one.

At the start of the 19th century, dresses became diaphanous, pockets disappeared, and the evening bag proper was born. Fashioned in the shape of a drooping blossom and known as a reticule, it was first carried by the empress Josephine, and quickly adopted by women at court and deep into the countryside. Soon elaborate bags in the shape of seashells, circular fans, and even pineapples were being crafted at home; the more ornate the bag, the more status bestowed upon the owner. Those with time to net silk and embroider Venetian beads all

*European,
c. 1910*

day had the leisure to play, and more importantly to court, all night. Jane Austen's descriptions of heroines quietly toiling over handmade lace bags provides no better image of the fierce social ambitions of young single ladies. A beautiful evening bag declared that you too could go to the ball.

The homemade bags of the 1830s and '40s, bedecked in dainty flowers, trimmed with velvet and poems in petit point, served as chaste and winsome self-portraits of their owners. As the century progressed, mass production and the hardened charms of professional beauties—opera singers, can-can dancers, and royal mistresses—influenced the evening bag. Feathers in great glossy clusters and heavy, ruched velvets were the blatantly erotic materials of the late-19th-century evening purse. What would Sigmund Freud have made

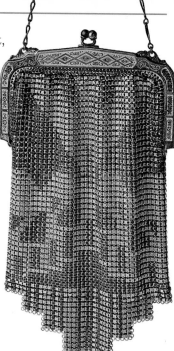

*Whiting and Davis, 1920s*

of the Belle Époque ostrich-trimmed opera bag with a tiny satin opening that gaped like a greedy mouth to reveal a circular mirror within? The image of the purse as a second sex began with the evening bag.

Linked forever with artifice and flirtation, an evening bag can be the size of a snow pea as long as it can hold a lipstick. In the 1920s cigarettes and rouge dictated the shape of the tango purse. Like the dresses of the era, deco metal mesh bags left little room for concealment. What could possibly be stored in the sinuous reptilian sheath of a Whiting and Davis silver mesh purse designed to be suspended from one finger?

*Valentino Garavani, 2001*

In the Great Depression, bags followed the lines of fashion closely. As '30s evening gowns were cut sheer to the body, so was the bag, with the clever bias-cut glass-beaded bag concealing a zipper within its folds. Tough times rarely touched the evening bag. When women couldn't buy them new they recycled old heirlooms, stitching modern straps to granny's Victorian velvets. During World War II a woman might have made do with a suede bag that went from day to night, but that bag had charisma and curves. Intrigue and disclosure were themes that informed '40s evening bags,

*Llewellyn, 1956*

with multipocketed interiors, hidden compartments, and a go-anywhere shoulder strap. This was the place femme fatales stashed their Lady Remingtons and Lucky Strikes. Such pragmatic privacy was brought up short with Dior's New Look, when the bag became

*Christian Dior
Fermoir, 1998*

decorative and beautifully frivolous all over again. The diamond-studded Lucite cocktail boxes of Wilardy and Patricia of Miami became as transparent as Cinderella's slipper, holding little more than powder and a prayer.

From this moment on, bags have reveled in being tiny, shiny, and cute, from the go-go bags of the '60s, clad in silver pailletes swinging from a bracelet hoop, to Oleg Cassini's slender cigar-shaped pochettes made for Jacqueline Kennedy, from fragile necklace bags of gold leather in the disco '70s to Judith Leiber's miser's bags studded with crystals. Today's impractical, tiny evening bag liberates by carrying less. Armed only with lipgloss and some lifesavers, the desk slave becomes a diva by night. Like a pair of spike heels, her evening bag declares to the world, "You take care of the details, baby, because tonight beauty is my full-time job."

*Natori, 2002*

AS RARE AS A BLACK TULIP,
a Judith Leiber minaudière
is an object of painstaking
luxury. Every Swarovsky
crystal is applied by hand
to the bag, which looks
like a jewel box.

JUDITH LEIBER, 2001

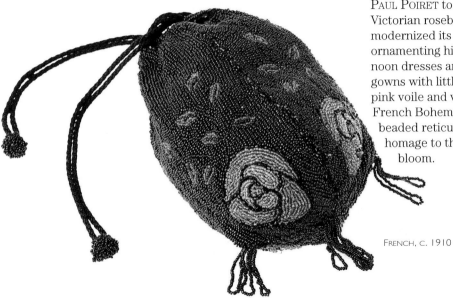

PAUL POIRET took the Victorian rosebud and modernized its form, ornamenting his afternoon dresses and evening gowns with little twists of pink voile and velvet. His French Bohemian beaded reticule pays homage to this modish bloom.

FRENCH, C. 1910

CLASSICAL ORNAMENT was the height of chic after the French revolution and was revived again in the early 20th century, when directoire dresses and gilded ornament dominated design.

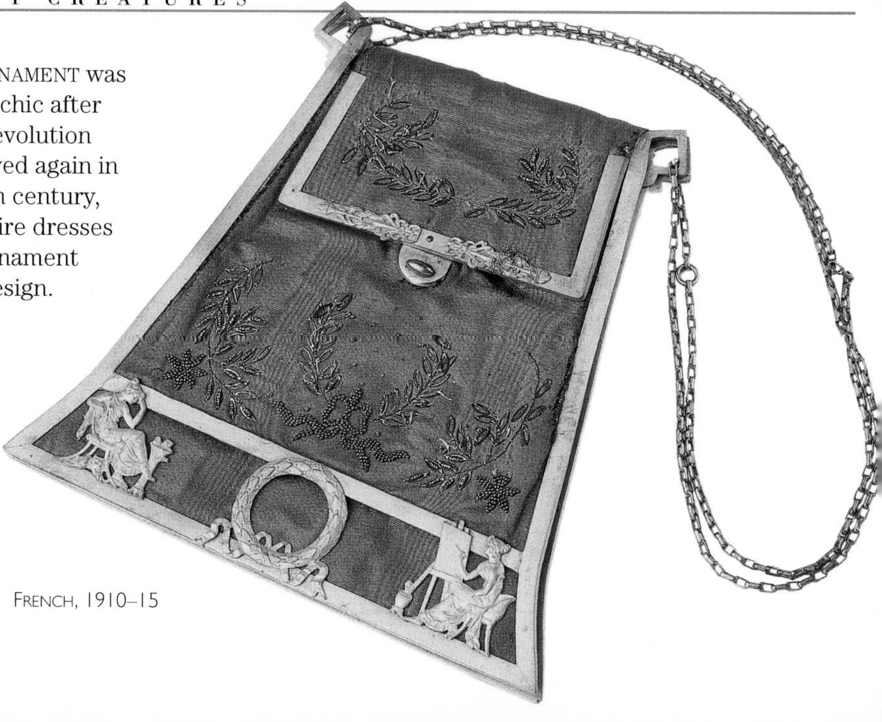

FRENCH, 1910–15

THE LUST FOR HANDMADE LACE, antique textiles, and embroidery at the turn of the last century was a reaction against industrialization. Women looked to a bag, often made in Venice or Florence, for the romance of handmade luxury and vintage splendor.

ITALIAN, C. 1910

ART NOUVEAU was marked
by organic curves and
undulating ornament.
Art deco was streamlined
and geometrically bold.
The beaded bags of the
late 1910s and early
'20s were a shameless
synthesis of the two.

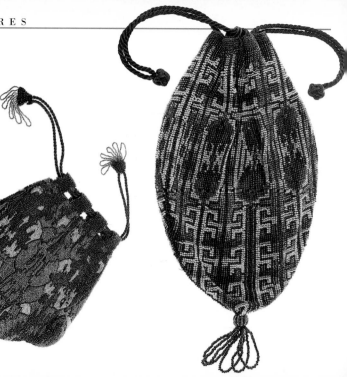

NEAR RIGHT: SAMSTAG'S
NEW YORK, 1920S;
RIGHT: FRENCH, 1920S

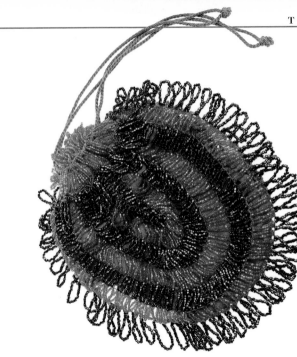

BAGS OFTEN MATCH SHOES, but in the '20s they echoed the dress, quivering with bugle beads and flapper fringe.

AMERICAN, 1920s

ANTHONY LUCIANO learned fine embroidery from his Sicilian grandmother. Carrying on a family tradition, he hand stitches duchess silk satin to vintage frames and ornaments them with Victorian beads and golden thread.

ANTHONY LUCIANO, 2001

ANTHONY LUCIANO, 2001

MADAME BUTTERFLY meets Metallica in Christian Dior's iconic evening bag. John Galliano for Dior takes a cue from Elsa Schiaparelli and then Zandra Rhodes, using the zipper as ornament and adding a soft little ruffle of petticoat tulle.

CHRISTIAN DIOR, 2001

"There is nothing I would like better than to make every woman look and feel like a duchess."

—*Christian Dior*

EGYPT WAS ALL THE RAGE when Claudette Colbert starred as Cleopatra in 1934, and the evening bag became suitably gilded and bejeweled.

FRENCH, 1936

INFLUENCED BY A DECADE OF DISCRETION and outlandish tap-dancing musicals, Walter Steiger fuses the two faces of the '30s in this metallic napa bag and shoe.

WALTER STEIGER, 2001

AN EMBARRASSMENT OF RICHES adorns Judith Leiber's pauper's purse, a collage of Tiffany stained glass and classic almoner style.

JUDITH LEIBER, 1991

NO PAUPER'S POUCH, this medieval-style evening bag by Cartier was cut from antelope skin and gilded with eighteen-karat gold.

CARTIER, 1930

THE SPARE GEOMETRY of industrial design was modernism's antidote to Victorian frippery. This crystal beaded bag, influenced by the Wiener Werkstadt, is little more than an envelope.

AUSTRIAN, 1920

WHEN JEWELS DROPPED off the dress they wound up on the handbag, the final resting place for theater and luxury in contemporary fashion. Handmade from semi-precious jewels and silver wire, this silk-lined box by Violette Nozières is brooch, bracelet, and bag in one.

VIOLETTE NOZIÈRES, 1999

LUXURY EVENING BAGS often borrow from the tailoring of the couture evening dress. Barbara Bolan's ruched and scalloped polished calf pochette has all the swagger of a neat '80s cocktail suit.

BARBARA BOLAN, 1984

VALENTINO GARAVANI makes the signature silk pleating of his evening gowns the dramatic focal point of his bag.

VALENTINO GARAVANI, 2001

# JUDITH LEIBER: THE SUCCESS OF EXCESS

T he designer of the world's glitziest evening bags whipped up her earliest creations from the cord binding found beneath old chairs in her mother's living room in prewar Budapest. Forced to improvise during the Nazi occupation, young Judith Leiber honed her skills in hard times. "Hitler put me in the handbag business," she once commented wryly, alluding to the fact that freshly liberated postwar Hungary was full of American women wanting pretty accessories. Leiber met the need and brought her skills to America in 1946 when she emigrated as the GI bride of Gerson Leiber, an American painter and longtime partner in her glittering empire. The young designer's high standards were initially frustrated by her first job at a five-dollar-bag factory that pumped out purses like "sheets of strudel." Deliverance came when she began

*James Bond bag, 1968*

*"Why not?" is Judith Leiber's two-word design philosophy.*

working for the more esteemed New York ateliers, especially Koret and Nettie Rosenstein. Leiber's first two decades in the bag trade deepened her passion for rare materials and hand-finished elegance. In 1963 she launched her own label.

Judith Leiber's early bags were feminine and sleek, and pulsed with an infusion of modernist art: a slender patent leather day bag with the curves of a Braque guitar, a pretty brown calfskin box bag with a dainty gold fob watch nestled in a front pocket the shape of a crescent moon, a little

*Blue silk tote with rhinestone ring handles, 1964*

white lunch box studded with nail heads. All of her bags displayed the hallmarks of long hours spent in European museums and her early guild training, which taught her to create "from the ground up." Leiber's bags of the late '60s combined whimsy with jet-set swagger. Her 007 bag featured a secret

*Chatelaine, 1967*

compartment in the base, her snakeskins were dyed emerald green, her clasps glittered with deco diamantés and hand-cast enamel.

Accomplished but eclectic, Leiber found her hallmark "look" by a happy accident. Although she set out to design a round-bottomed, solid metallic evening bag in the shape of a medieval coin purse (a chatelaine), her first prototype came back from Italy imperfect. To cover a patch of botched gold plating, Leiber scattered rhinestones across the bag's base. The result was the first Judith Leiber metal bag, the Chatelaine, a precursor to her most famous evening bag, the minaudière. Inspired by the solid art deco box bags of Van Cleef and Arpels and

*Hillary's cat, Barbara's pug, the first ladies' pets in rhinestones*

fabricated in gold plate, the Chatelaine was made for long enchanted evenings and short black cocktail dresses. "We made 300 of them in 1967, and didn't know enough to get it copyrighted and a million have been copied since. My logic at the time was why should a woman keep her solid gold handbag in the vault? Why can't glamour be more accessible?" *Accessible* is not the first adjective that springs to mind when describing a butterfly studded with Swarovsky crystals, but Leiber's intent has always been fun. Deluxe, irreverent, expensive fun.

*Gift box minaudière, 1993*

The glittery little Fabergé egg–shaped bags beloved today by socialites, eccentric pop stars, and first ladies hatched in the mid-'70s and grew from there. Influenced by a love of exotic bibelot—decorative boxes, Chinese ceramics, and sculpture—Leiber built a menagerie of bag shapes, each one presenting its own technical challenges. From the first teardrop-shaped minaudière there evolved a line of animals, flowers, and box bags tricked out like Tiffany stained glass. Each one was hand studded with up to seven thousand individual Swarovsky crystals and lined in gold kid. Holding a crystal-coated piglet with black onyx nostrils in one hand, the designer smiles gently and declares, "I have made crazy bags, some not that crazy, and some medium crazy. You have to have some that are kind of kooky." Some indeed. Leiber's sculpted polar bears and encrusted money bags became '80s icons of gilded opulence. Bridging the gap between a deco-rative art object and a fashion accessory, the minaudière

reestablished the expensive statement bag in American fashion and made a place for luxury with humor. Not since the 1920s had luxury bags been so decadently witty.

Twenty years later and nostalgic for the age of big hair and bright baby bags, the minaudière has enjoyed a massive revival since the millennium. Perhaps we want to appear impractical again, to look as if we'd stepped out of a pumpkin instead of a subway car. Judith Leiber's belief that a lady need only carry a lipstick, a handkerchief, and a hundred-dollar bill is expressed in her diminutive, jewel-like bags that serve as an antidote to the schlep, an abnegation of responsibility at its most glamorous.

*Certain socialites in Texas line up their Leiber bags as centerpieces for gala dinner parties.*

THE FLAPPER'S MINIMAL tango purse, swinging nonchalantly from the wrist, was often little more than a glorified compact, squeezing in powder, rouge, and a lipstick.

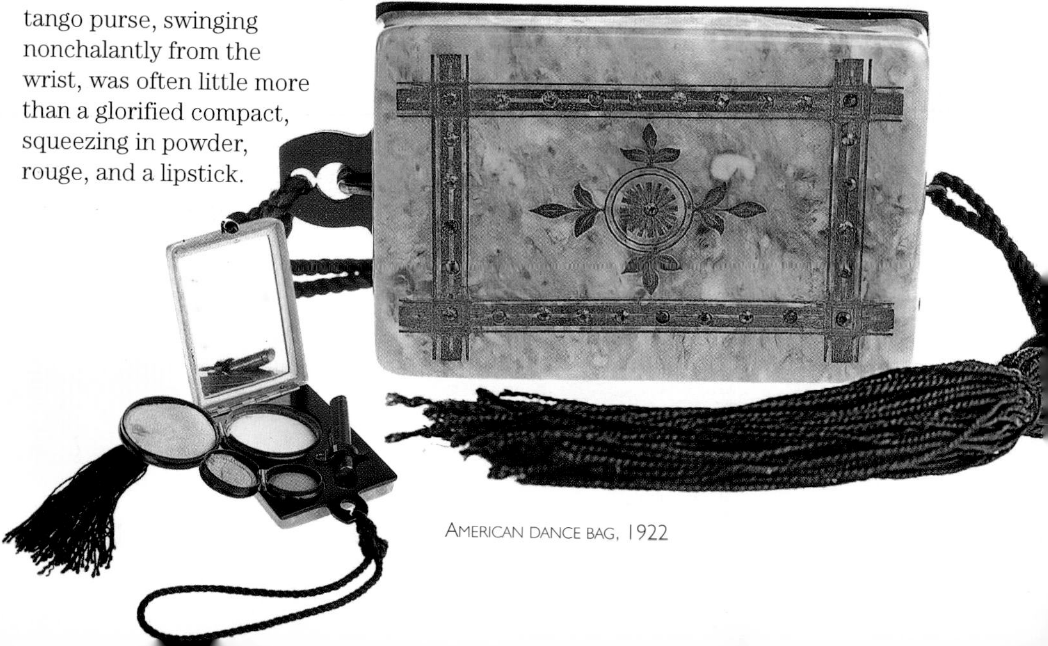

AMERICAN DANCE BAG, 1922

BELLE ÉPOQUE FASHION borrowed heavily from the salty style of the cabaret and dancehall stars of Montmartre. Gaping open to reveal a greedy little satin mouth, this ostrich-trimmed opera bag evokes Flaubert's famous bon mot: "Exuberance is better than taste."

FRENCH, C. 1900

GILDED LEATHER was the passport to style in the 1930s, but in the '60s it had to be metal mesh, androgynous, futuristic, and hanging on a chunky chain.

WHITING AND DAVIS
GOLD MESH BAG, 1970

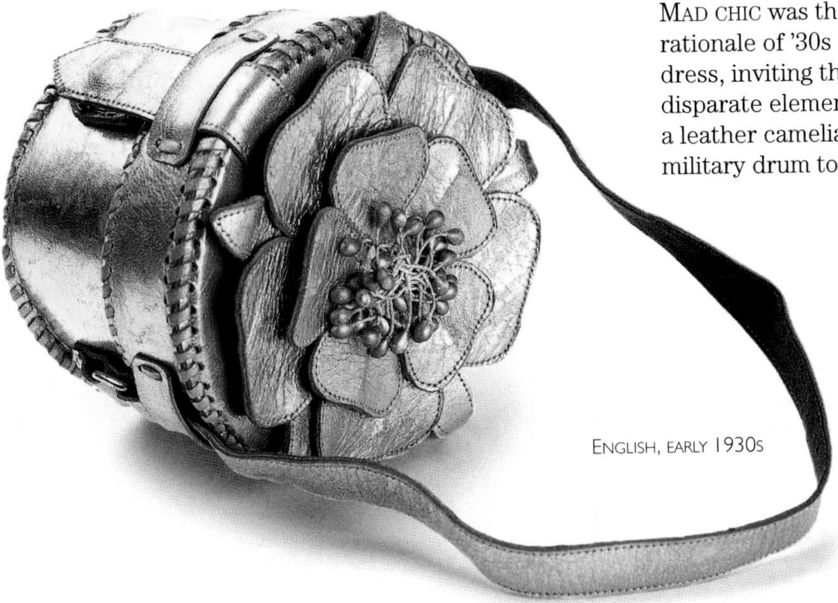

MAD CHIC was the rationale of '30s evening dress, inviting the disparate elements of a leather camelia and a military drum to dance.

ENGLISH, EARLY 1930s

REVLON'S FIRE AND ICE lipstick. Chevrolet's red Thunderbird. The blazing crimson beaded bags of Belgium and France. Fifties style was red in everything but its politics.

DELILL, 1950s

**"When in doubt wear red."**
*—Bill Blass*

FERRAGAMO, 1994

LIKE A GASH of red lipstick
or a pair of spike heels,
the red handbag spells
seduction.

NATORI, 2002

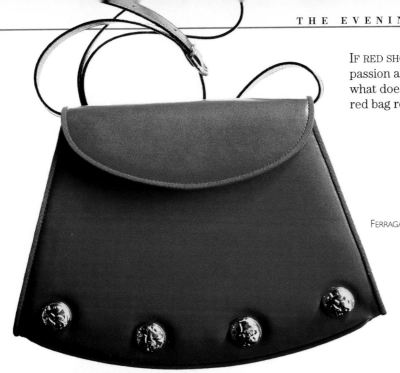

IF RED SHOES signify passion and danger, what does a bright red bag represent?

FERRAGAMO, 1991

THE FINGER PURSE came
into vogue in the 1890s,
when all things romantic
and medieval, including
the silver chatelaine,
were being revived.

SILVER FINGER PURSE, C. 1915

WITH AN EXOTIC NAME and a theatrical shape, the Delysia vanity compact bag was shaped like an amphora and held cosmetics in its discreet compartments.

WHITING AND DAVIS, 1924

CINDERELLA'S SLIPPER finds its match in this clear plastic box festooned with rhinestones. Such transparency reflects the decorative and objectified femininity of the '50s, as opposed to the secrecy and implicit power of the locked handbag.

PATRICIA OF MIAMI, 1950

Princess proportions in the '90s shrank the satin Fermoire bag to the size of a pea. The baby bag declared the luxury of having to carry nothing but attitude and cash.

Christian Dior, 1998

PEAKING IN POPULARITY
in the '50s, leopard and
tiger prints promised
primal pleasures for
prim suburbanites.
Jean Paul Gaultier's
interpretation is
created with a
recycled vintage
coat and a "Me Jane"
bracelet.

JEAN PAUL GAULTIER, 1998

**"Elegance is refusal."**
—*Diana Vreeland*

French boucle pochette
and netted gloves, 1930

Working the room is about all the labor an 18th-century lady did with her silk work bag. Ostensibly for knitting, they soon became popular accessories for evening, stuffed with cosmetics, fans, and a little bit of handwork for the sake of appearance.

American, late 18th century

"Meanwhile, to heighten all her charms
The work-bag dangled on her arms:
    The very bag that British Belles
Bear on their arms at Tunbridge Wells."
    —*The London Magazine, 1764*

FRENCH, C.1890

ARTS AND CRAFTS DESIGNERS
adored folkloric ornament
and bold organic forms,
creating bags of rare and
peculiar beauty.

GERMAN, 1910

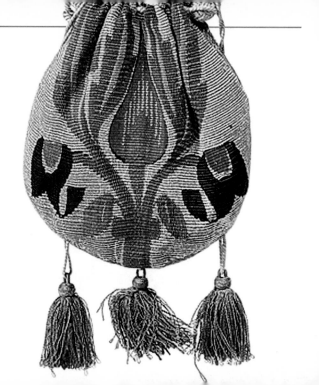

IN THIS RETRO CONFECTION, Bakelite, taffeta, and beads, the materials of three different decades, form a design pastiche of the dance bag from 1900 to 1930.

JILL STUART, 1996

GLAMOUR IS A MATTER OF
PHYSICS. Weight creates
movement, and strands of
heavy glass beads create
a dancing mermaid's tail.
This beaded bag recalls
the era of the tea dance
and Irene Castle's
fringed-hem tango
gowns.

FRENCH WRIST BAG, C. 1910

"The accessory is always a delicate balance between good and bad taste. In other words a handbag may either make or break an outfit."

—*Valentino Garavani*

VALENTINO GARAVANI, 2001

THE BABY CLUTCH, worn
with a skinny tee, heels,
and jeans, became a
downtown uniform at the
end of the 20th century.

LOUIS VUITTON
POCHETTE, 2001

"It seems uptown girls like their bags to coordinate with their shoes while downtown girls could probably care less."

—*John Ross, Patch*

PATCH, 2001

HEAVY ORIENTAL CLASPS and rich antique textiles were popular in Italy and France in the early '20s. Created with precious jewels and now-priceless damask, these clutches mimicked the opulence of Byzantium and 18th-century Venice.

FRENCH, 1915–25

SEQUINS WERE THE
WORKING GIRL'S ANSWER
to costly glass beads
during the Depression.
This little Belgian bag
may have been worn with
a sexy matching beret.

BELGIAN, 1930S

"I find that it is vital to have at least one handbag for each of the ten types of social occasion: Very Formal, Not So Formal, Just a Teensy Bit Formal, Informal But Not That Informal, Every Day, Every Other Day, Day Travel, Night Travel, Theater, and Fling."
—*Miss Piggy*

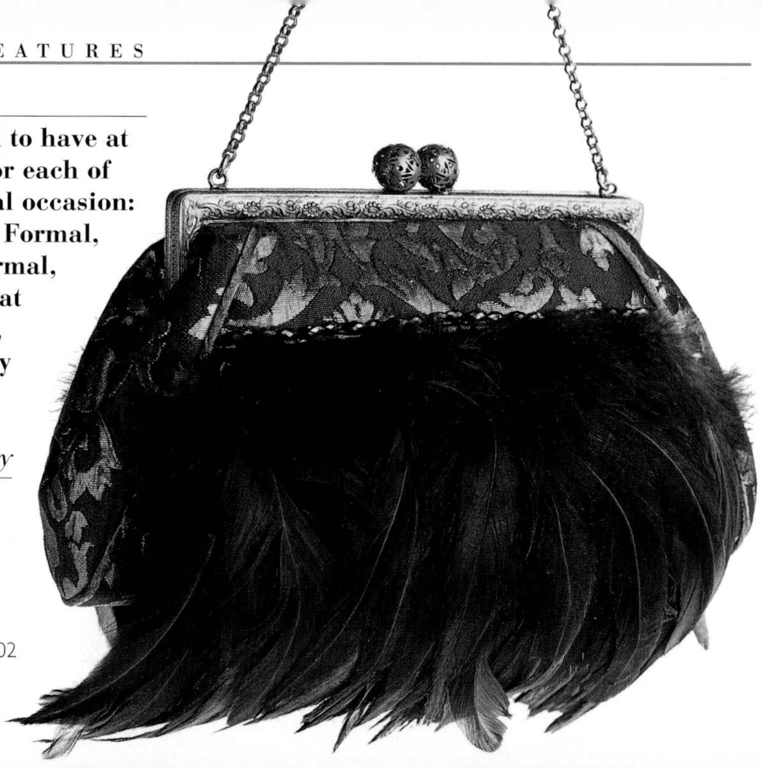

ANTHONY LUCIANO, 2002

EVENING BEAUTY PIVOTS on delicate detail: the two tiny swans that secure the chain of a vintage clasp and the fragile dusting of glass beads that trace a swirl of screen-printed flowers.

BOCHAVAR ACCESSORIES, 2001

SHALL WE DANCE?
Two spectacularly
swell evening bags
don tiara, bow tie,
and tails.

VALENTINO GARAVANI,
MARABOU FEATHER,
SWAROVSKY CRYSTAL,
AND SILK BRACELET BAG,
2000

WALTER STEIGER, BLACK SUEDE
AND GOLD KID, 2000

PSYCHEDELIC VELVET, tangerine leather, and a faux gold cane handle scream rock aristocracy in this jaunty baby bag by Pucci.

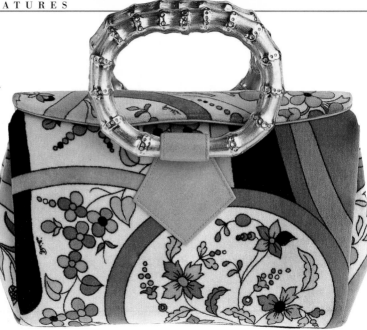

PUCCI, 1960s

IN THE '60s, BAGS HAD TO SWING, literally. These Italian disco bags were knockoffs of the more elite creations of Courrèges and Paco Rabanne.

ITALIAN, C. 1960s

ACCESSORY AS ARMOR and handbag
as fetish—Jean Paul Gaultier forged
his gladiator-style clutch from
beaten gilded metal, to be worn
as a hand-held amulet.

JEAN PAUL GAULTIER, 1998

**"When in doubt, overdress."**
—*Vivienne Westwood*

*American metal mesh bag with silver ball trim, 1910*

# THE METAL MESH BAG

W hat a lovely contradiction is metal mesh: a slinky sheer veil made from the stuff of armor, the most fluid and organic lines from the most industrial of materials, and the look of lingerie in a fabric tougher than nails. The first mesh bags were made by gold- and silversmiths in the 1820s and framed with precious stones. Toward the end of the 19th century, when all things medieval were in vogue, silver mesh finger purses and small mesh coin purses designed to hang from a chatelaine were introduced. Until the

*American solid silver bag, marked "Merry Christmas, 1900"*

*American enamel mesh, 1920s*

*Whiting and Davis, 1920s*

20th century, mesh had to be linked entirely by hand, a process that made the bags rare and coveted luxuries. In 1908 A. C. Pratt patented the mesh machine, and the delicate metal bags became an affordable indulgence.

By the teens, the American company Whiting and Davis dominated the market, with hand-etched silver frames, elegant silhouettes, and clever marketing. Attracting foreign talent (Paul Poiret and Elsa Schiaparelli both designed for Whiting and Davis) and constantly updating their styles, the company kept the mesh bag current for almost a century. In the '20s, a filmy little

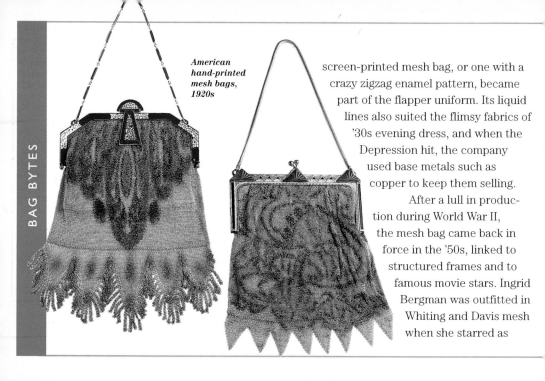

*American hand-printed mesh bags, 1920s*

screen-printed mesh bag, or one with a crazy zigzag enamel pattern, became part of the flapper uniform. Its liquid lines also suited the flimsy fabrics of '30s evening dress, and when the Depression hit, the company used base metals such as copper to keep them selling. After a lull in production during World War II, the mesh bag came back in force in the '50s, linked to structured frames and to famous movie stars. Ingrid Bergman was outfitted in Whiting and Davis mesh when she starred as

*Egyptian-style vanity bag with a compact-lid, 1925*

Joan of Arc, and Jane Russell slunk around in a twenty-one-pound gilt mesh cocktail dress in the 1951 film *Macao*. Mesh got its groove back in the '70s in the form of halter tops and matching disco bags. Though still in production and highly popular with everyone's grandma, contemporary mesh is no match for the extraordinary dance and evening bags of the '20s, those delicate sheaths that shimmer like a butterfly's wing.

*American gold mesh bag, late 1940s*

VATICAN VELVETS AND beaten gold were the stuff of Roberta di Camerino's luxurious box bags of the '50s. The Venetian designer brought a theatrical Renaissance sensibility to the cocktail hour.

ROBERTA DI CAMERINO, 1959

LIKE A FRESHLY POWDERED FACE, an evening bag, sets out into the night full of promise and self-contained allure. Three cocktails, two taxi rides, and several dances later, Cinderella unravels, loosening her secrets and lowering her guard.

FERRAGAMO, 1991

FOREVER FRESH, this bouquet of rosebuds is hand-carved and hand-painted on the inside of a hard acrylic shell, creating the illusion of a frozen garden.

JOYCE FRANCIS, 2002

ARTFUL COLLAGE,
fantastic fragments,
and scattered sequins
are framed on bag and
shoe, '60s style radically
updated.

CHRISTIAN LOUBOUTIN,
2001

ORIENTAL THEMES: calligraphy, bamboo, and designs inspired by lacquer work were the last word in chic in the late '50s. More recent takes on the theme have found wit in the Chinese take-out box and the silk frogging of a cheong sam.

JAPANESE, 1960

LULU GUINNESS,
2001

THE EVENING BAG AS ART was taken literally in the 1950s. Fragonard's *Girl on a Swing* is the perfect painting for a night of flirtation.

ITALIAN, EARLY 1950s

PHOTOGRAPHY ON LEATHER creates a strange illusion of a bag's interior revealed. Opera gloves, ribbons, and mementos hint at nostalgic romance.

DONNA MAY BOLINGER, 2002

BEADED BAGS HAVE ALWAYS been beloved for night, catching the light and creating a subtle gleam of ornament. The royal blue filigree of a Cartier bag was created to match a lapis lazuli clasp.

CARTIER, 1930s

BELGIUM AND FRANCE exported fine beaded bags to America in the late '50s and early '60s. Detailed and restrained, they complemented the minimalist cocktail hour look—high heels and a silk sheath.

BELGIAN, 1950s–60s

SIMPLICITY WAS KEY to modern '60s design, with brilliant color and subtle textural detail replacing '50s razzle-dazzle.

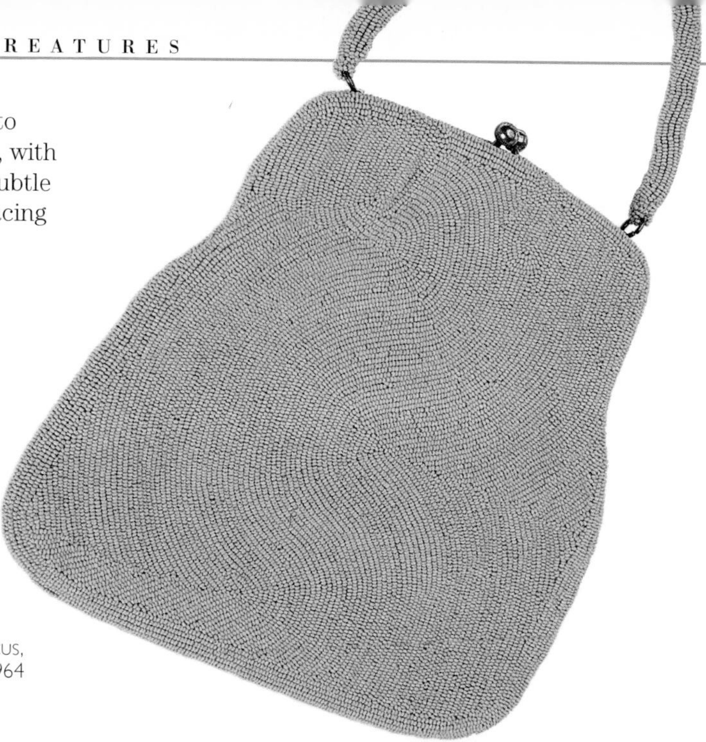

BELGIAN, FOR NIEMAN MARCUS, 1964

THE INTENSE LUXURY of a bag woven completely from coral beads looks deceptively simple. A classic case of discreet riches, '30s style.

FRENCH, 1930

Fusing folk wisdom with frivolous luxury, this bag combines Granny's knitted trims with candy-pink python. The deliberate contrast between sophisticated hardware, logo, and crafty trims typifies hippie deluxe style.

Fendi, 2000

HANDMADE POCKETBOOKS hark back to 19th-century crazy quilts and the romantic palette of the Bloomsbury artists.

PATTY BOZZA, 2000

THE POCHETTE has mutated in size and shape since
its birth in the '20s. By the '40s, evening clutches like
this silk nightclub number had grown larger to suit
the prevailing utility of wartime.

SILK CORD
POCHETTE,
LATE 1940S

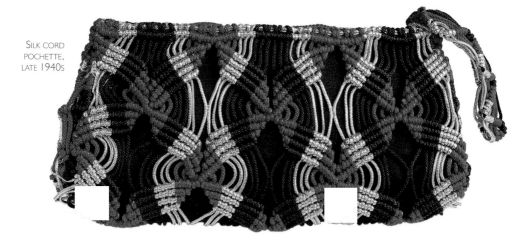

By the '80s, the hand-held classic was worn discreetly small again, tucked against the body like a second palm.

Barbara Bolan,
1981

GLAMOUR IS A MATCHING SHOE AND BAG—
and look how they change in a decade.
The war bride starlet wore a sturdy
sequined and beaded bag bedecked
with bow and chunky shoulder strap.

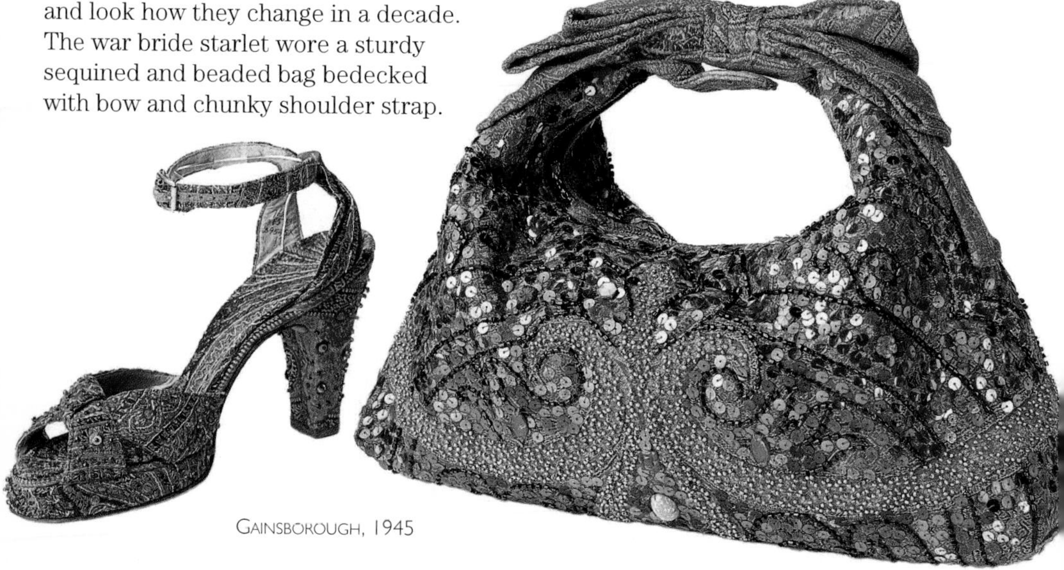

GAINSBOROUGH, 1945

BY THE EARLY '50s, the platform has become a slinky mule and the bag a lean streak of modernist silk with a skinny strap.

JOSEPH LA ROSE, 1955

EVENING HAS ALWAYS
come dressed in velvet.
For Roberta di Camerino
the fabric is a signature,
a symbol of Italian artisan
splendor.

ROBERTA DI CAMERINO FOR
NEIMAN MARCUS, 1967

THE CHARM BRACELET
chain makes a purse
more precious.

ROBERTA DI CAMERINO,
1979

THE LUNCH BOX AND THE SCHOOL BAG make playful models for evening bags that look like toys.

COURRÈGES, 2000

"... this brilliantly
bourgeoise bag, the
leather equivalent of
a yapping chihuahua."
—*Mimi Spencer,
on the Lady Dior bag*

CHRISTIAN DIOR, LADY DIOR, 1989

LUXURY NEEDS to find ways to subvert itself to stay compelling. It does this through incongruous materials, uncomfortable associations, and aggressive iconography.

VALENTINO GARAVANI, 2001

REGIMENTAL REGALIA has a seductive hold over fashion—so much so that in recent times luxury style has developed militant tendencies.

CHANEL, 2001

EXTRAVAGANCE IS THE HALLMARK of a bag for night. Studded with crystals, a great evening bag doesn't require an occasion. It simply becomes one.

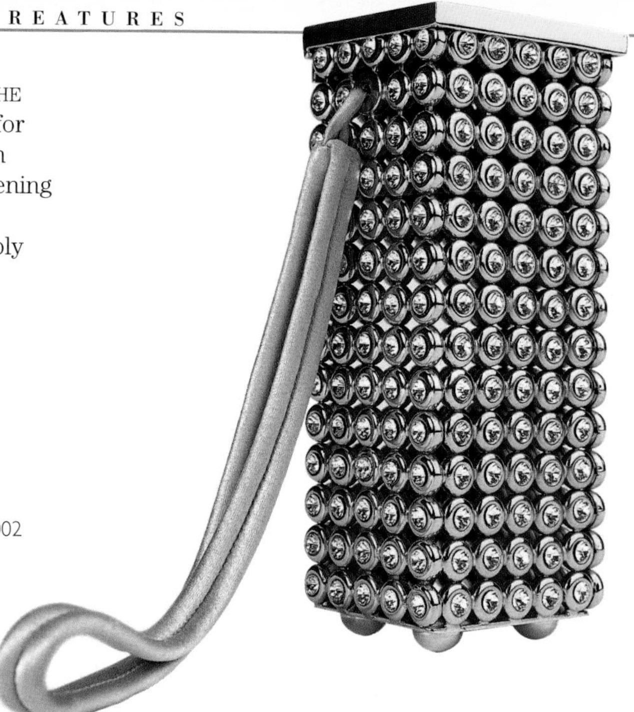

BADGLEY MISCHKA, 2002

"I loathe narcissism but I approve of vanity."
—*Diana Vreeland*

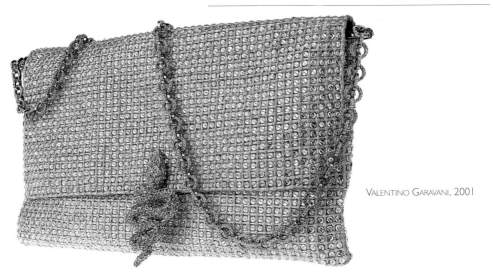

VALENTINO GARAVANI, 2001

"Fashion, even anti-fashion, is forever. It's the only way we can become the characters we wish to be."

—*Christian Lacroix*

CHRISTIAN LACROIX COUTURE,
CRYSTAL TEDDY BEAR BAG, 2002

# three

# Sculptural Chic: Shape & Structure

Of all fashion accessories, the handbag presents the greatest opportunity to create a singular sculptural object. More than a hat, which must compete with the face, more than shoes, which must dance in pairs, the bag stands alone. Austere and dramatic on the horizon of a restaurant table or a back-lit bar, a great-shaped bag speaks for its owner in bold, decisive terms. No matter how messy or ill-defined its contents, a sleek handbag silhouette casts a powerful shadow.

Social change is always announced by a radical transformation in the shape of things.

*Gucci, 2002; Previous page: Natori, 2002*

In the case of bags, the stripping of ornament, the swelling of
the belly, or the sprouting of oversized handles were always
signs of the times. War makes bags bigger, boom times
make them smaller. Modern art has made them simpler,
and feminism has given them functionality, compartments,
and sturdy fittings. Unlike hemlines, however, the silhouette
of the bag is not always the most reliable social barometer.
Some of the most radical-looking bags in history were
designed in the most conservative political climates:
the fascist '30s and the McCarthyist '50s. Revolutions,
both sexual and political, have been accessorized by
distinctly informal and free-form bags: the woven
hippie shoulder bags of the 1960s and '70s used
rustic textures, handwoven textiles, and amorphic,
sinuous shapes—bohemians have never loved the
structured handbag.

*Wilardy, 1954*

*Jill Stuart,*
*1980*

*Walter Steiger,*
*2001*

Bags have their own geography (the '30s pochette bag went east to west, and a tall bag is known as a north/south), and a geometry with strong emotional associations. Certain conventional shapes are reassuring: for example, a triangular bag looks like the peaked roof on a storybook house. A perfectly square bag suggests a book or a gift box. A round bag worn at the hip is like an ancient food-gathering basket, and a spherical backpack can feel like offspring. When Vivienne Westwood created a buttock-shaped "fanny pack" out of Louis Vuitton's monogram canvas and strapped it to a model's hips, she demonstrated the subversive force of a bag with a suggestive shape. Sculpted bags, when worn in dramatic relief against the body, evoke the ghosts of extinct fashions: the gauntlet, the girdle, or in Westwood's case, the bustle.

*Vivienne Westwood for Louis Vuitton, 1996*

The evolution of materials has also influenced the shape of the bag. As craftsmen became more skilled with leather and metalwork in the Middle Ages, bags gained more structure, and with that came a growing relationship between the bag and art and architecture. A 16th-century purse shaped like a fleur-de-lis crest was influenced by heraldic shields and the interior ornament of the Renaissance palazzo. An early 18th-century sculpted leather bag in the shape of a seashell may

*Ply, 2001*

have been inspired by the fascination with chinoiserie and rococo garden follies. By the Victorian era, bags, bustles, and crinolines grew unwieldy, and the little leather handbag became streamined and simplified for travel. By 1910, the industrial revolution had led to a cleft between bags for night and bags for day. In bags for day, the innovations of the mechanical age were enjoyed, whereas for evening all that was mass produced, metallic, and hard was rejected in favor of hand embroidery, artisan cloth, and beadwork. Pioneered by suffragettes and soldiers, the frankly masculine, square, and abbreviated shoulder bag of the 1900s was coveted for both its modernity and its sheer practicality.

Geometric form became more important with the rise of modernism, in which ornament was eliminated to the point where the object's form was all that was left. Sonia Delaunay's bags of the 1920s were as square as an abstract painting and were themselves a canvas for her musings on color and composition. The long envelope-shaped pochette bags of the '30s stripped the bag back to its essential function: a

*Koret, 1950*

large pocket with sturdy front clasp. Hermès spearheaded the look, and the firm continues to sell the same style almost unchanged. Minimal styles with strong plain frames tend to endure. Most of the bags we have today (the bucket, the hobo, the zip-topped tote, and the triangular structured handbag with a top handle) all originated before World War II.

By the late '40s industrial design and a growing fascination with public works and architecture rendered the handbag monumentally large and structurally adventurous: concertina bags that

*Llewellyn,*
*1950*

opened on a diagonal, box bags stacked with secret compartments, clasps made of sliding metal panels and riveted mesh. All looked like they might have been designed by Howard Roark, Ayn Rand's megalomaniac architect in *The Fountainhead*. By the '50s modern materials had caught up with the fantastic visions of designers. The plastic handbag was born out of wartime technology; some of its designers were manufacturers of World War II plastic parts, and its designs broke all fashion rules. Beginning in the late '40s and early '50s, designers like Wilardy began to use the new plastic, Lucite, to create some of the most inventively shaped bags ever seen. Soon the simple Lucite box took on bizarre shapes (the pail, the trapezoid, the hatbox, the coffin, the beehive) and was embellished with rhinestones, pearls, shells, and artificial flowers. Hard-edged, slick, and stiffly stylized, these bags put sculptural form and dramatic lines above all other practical concerns. Like high-maintenance

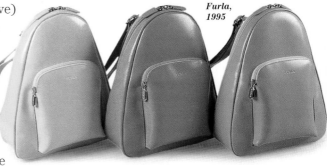

*Furla,
1995*

starlets, they were expensive, carried little, and tarnished easily (contemporary collectors obsess over scratches), but looked fabulous. Inspired by everything from costume jewels to futuristic car dashboards, the masters of plastic—such as Rialto, Florida Handbags, and Llewellyn—took their medium to its limits, creating rippled lids, dramatic elliptical boxes, daggerlike clasps, and savage curves. Sublime but short lived, the rigidity of high-glamour plastic bags held little appeal to the next generation, who were bringing back sari-silk shoulder bags and delicate baskets from Asia.

*Chanel 2005 bag, 1999*

Structured, minimal, and dramatically shaped bags returned when postmodernism revived the most playful elements of the '50s and the most erotic pockets of surrealism. When Philippe Starck gave his cartoonlike furniture pet names and Issey Miyake put Grace Jones in a vacuum-formed hard latex corset, the handbag had occasion to become a toy, a sculptural object, and a conversation piece all over again. In this century, young industrial designers are turning their hand to redefining the bag and its shape, creating backpacks shaped like beetle wings and fastenings that spring shut with the pull of a toggle. Lagerfeld for Chanel carved the 2005 bag into a new curve, giving it the look of a Teletubbie with the mumps.

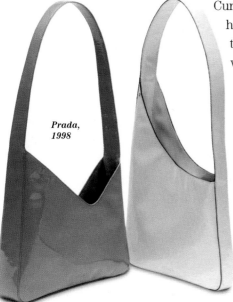

*Prada,*
*1998*

Curves in everything from tea kettles to car hoods heralded the millennium, and handbags joined the ovoid fold, cast in the shape of planets and worn over the shoulder like gigantic doughnuts.

The optimism that suggests that a bag can carry a woman into the future goes hand in hand with the notion that modernity is a perpetual process of reduction and invention. Most bags today feature a home for a mobile phone and a Palm Pilot. One day soon we will be able to compress a virtual office into the place where a compact once fit. Corbusier's notion of less being more applies well to the most pragmatically intimate of female accessories. If anything is a machine for living, it is the handbag.

A BAG IN THE HAND
is worth two on the
shoulder. The return
of the luxuriously long
clutch in the '50s was
a reaction against
utility, rationing,
and the stodgy
style of
wartime.

NEIMAN MARCUS, 1950s

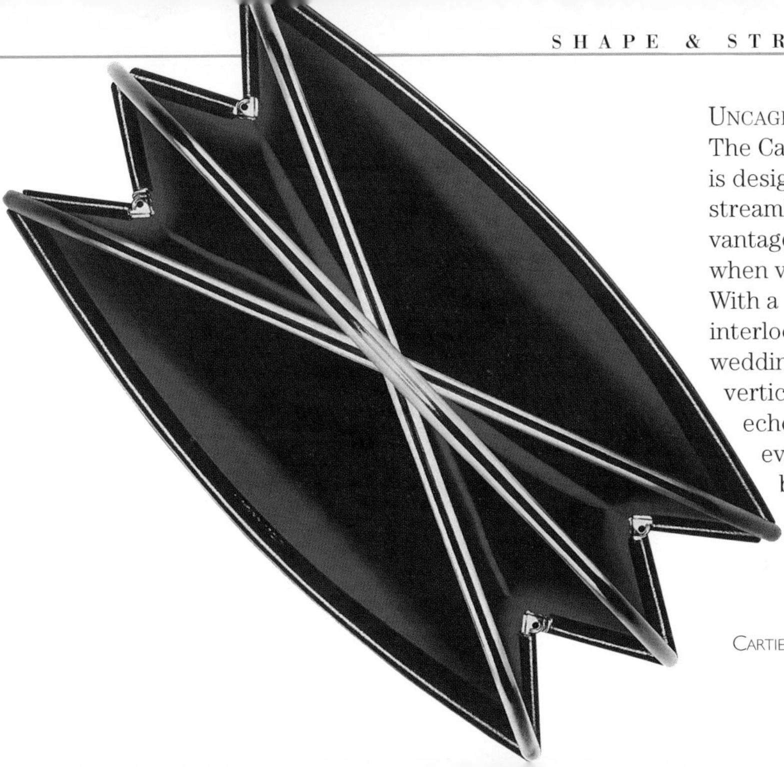

UNCAGE MY HEART.
The Cage de Cartier
is designed to appear
streamlined from every
vantage point, especially
when viewed from above.
With a handle that
interlocks like a Russian
wedding ring, the slim
vertical lines of the bag
echo the sleekest
evening bags created
by the house in the
'20s and '30s.

CARTIER, 2001

DUTCH DESIGNER Jan
Jansen called his shoe
bag the "flying wedge,"
creating a futuristic
fantasy and sexy
fetish in one.

JAN JANSEN, 1989

GEORGE RUFF, 1928

TRAINS, PLANES, AND AUTOMOBILES were popular motifs for the figural pochettes of the 1930s that sat like snug little toys against the sober suits of the era.

PLEATS, PRETTY PLEASE. Japanese designer Issey Miyake tests the kinetic energy of fabrics by pleating and cutting cloth like a sculptor. His accordion bag made of wool is unusually wide and dances against the body.

ISSEY MIYAKE, 2001

STRAIGHT OUT OF *I LOVE LUCY,* Jill Stuart's handbag designs for her Japanese boutiques adopt a playful, almost cartoonlike character with outsized bows, retro silver chains, and a perky color scheme.

JILL STUART, 2001

Hollywood came to Germany after World War II, when the Marshall Plan, an initiative to boost the European economy, gave modern materials to industry. Germans had never before seen pastel leathers like these, sold as the "Hollywood Series."

Goldpfeil, 1948, 1949

"I want to invent new ways of making clothes in new materials, with new shapes and fashion accessories that are up to date with the changing ways of life."
—*Mary Quant, 1966*

MARY QUANT, 1966

A TRIPLE-DECKER BAG on a jaunty Bakelite bracelet handle was thrifty shopping, '30s-style.

AMERICAN, 1930s

MODERN RIFFS ON THE VICTORIAN MISER BAG allowed for a more generous shape and a more glamorous execution. This large suede miser purse features a natty clock face and easy-access clasps at either end.

ENGLISH, 1919

PIERRE BALMAIN'S interpretation of the miser echoes the fullness of his couture gowns. Cut from black velvet and dusted with rhinestones, the bag seems more a magnificent bustle than a housewife's coin purse.

PIERRE BALMAIN, 1940s

A CONCERTINA CANE BASKET
that folded flat could
probably hold no more
than a sweater and a silk
scarf, but the novelty of
its jutting spine and eco-
nomical simplicity gave it
charm.

AMERICAN, LATE 1940s

ACCORDION BAGS WERE popular in the late '40s and early '50s, both for their novelty and for their utility. Carrying one couldn't have been comfortable, but the rewards were the many divine little compartments.

AMERICAN, 1940s

CLEVER CLASPS AND OPENINGS
relied on smooth, interlocking
geometry. The mouth of this
black suede evening bag draws
open on pivoting embossed
panels that slide on a metal track.

B. ALTMAN, 1940s

THE MOST COSTLY GOLDEN BOX compact bags of the 1930s were made by Boucheron. This chic copy covered with gold plate and rhinestone rubies popped open with a flick of its elegantly concealed catch.

TURKISH, EARLY 1930s

GRACEFUL AS A GUITAR, this Lucite bag had full-figured charm. Sculptured '50s bags often featured a waistline and "hips," homage to the va-va-voom stars of the day.

FLORIDA HANDBAGS, 1955–56

ALTARS, MONUMENTS, and mausoleums to makeup—these were the dramatic impressions made by mid-century Lucite box bags.

RIALTO PAGODA, 1952

A SCULPTURE WITH BOUNCE is one way to describe the elastic elegance of the Ply Toggle bag. The structural leather shell can be drawn tight when its wool interior is ruched together or opened wide with a tug on the toggle. The effect is like an urban papoose, snug and sleek at the same time.

PLY, 2001

**"A season without Yves Saint Laurent is like a season without God."**

—*Hebe Dorsey*

YVES SAINT LAURENT made the first modern art mini when he put a Mondrian painting on a dress. Inspired by Yves Kline with a dash of Barnet Newman, this bag celebrates the beauty of abstract art.

YVES SAINT LAURENT, 1975

THIS ONE BITES. A suede '40s bag has a glamorous set of jaws, all the more devouring with their lipstick-red lining. No wonder some men associate the mysterious interior of the handbag with danger.

AMERICAN, 1940S

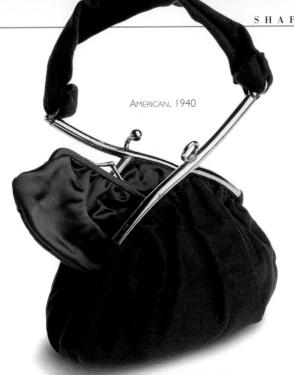

AMERICAN, 1940

INDUSTRIAL DESIGN innovation and modernist jewelry both inform the clever, interlocking clasp on this silk evening purse from 1940.

THE BAG AS BOUDOIR is the perfect accomplice for applying makeup in public. The slick little antelope bag worked like a portable powder room for modern women on the hop from club to cocktail lounge.

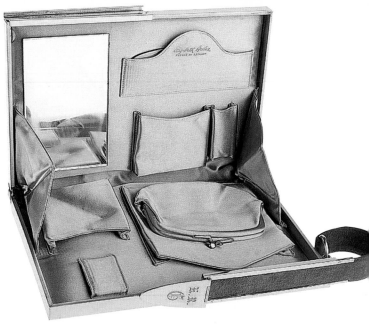

ELIZABETH ARDEN, EARLY 1930s

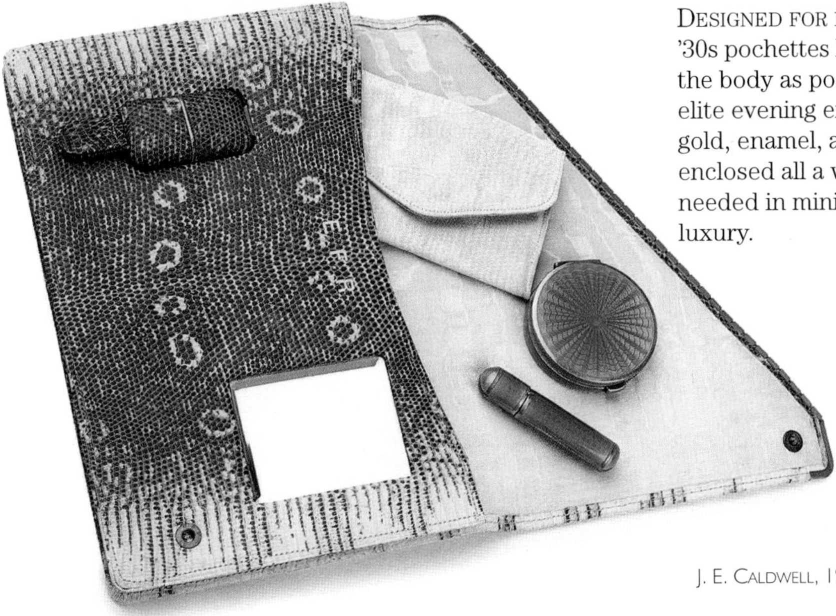

DESIGNED FOR DISCRETION, '30s pochettes lay as flat to the body as possible. This elite evening envelope in gold, enamel, and python enclosed all a woman needed in miniaturized luxury.

J. E. CALDWELL, 1930

THE POCHETTE STYLE originated in the 18th century, when men and woman carried documents in envelopes of leather and silk. These evolved into a solid framed enamel or tortoiseshell purse in the Edwardian era, and reached their stride as a perfectly minimal handbag in the '20s, when unadorned simplicity was the key to chic.

TURKISH EMBOSSED LEATHER, 18TH CENTURY

FRENCH AND GERMAN, 1900–20

A BAG IN THE HAND . . . Early enamel and shell pochettes led the march toward minimal style.

## WILL HARDY: THE LORD OF LUCITE

The most extravagant sculptural bags of the 1950s were created by an extravagant man. At his professional peak Will Hardy lived larger than Elvis, collecting flashy cars, sporting silk suits, and creating handbags studded with rhinestones, colored glass, and the fanciest filigree hardware. Hardy's love affair with plastic began at the age of twelve, when he built a birdhouse out of Lucite. Continuing to experiment with the material while studying industrial design and mechanical drafting in his late teens, Hardy joined Handbag Specialties, his father's family business, in 1948, and immediately shifted the company's design focus away from metal.

*Wilardy Rocket, 1953*

Hardy's vision was to create the indestructible handbag, a bag as strong as an automobile that would last forever. "In the 50s, plastic was being hyped as the material of the future and that prophesy has come true," he says. "Other plastics yellow but Lucite is timeless and the clear surface keeps it's color."

*The award-winning designer, 1954.*

"I added two handles to a hard plastic jewelry box and it looked great as a bag, so I took it from there."
— *Will Hardy*

Wilardy (he elided his name to give it a catchy, commercial ring) developed a form of Lucite that was both glossy and tough, and stuck with it. Hand cast and heat soldered together, the Lucite bag was expensive to produce and carried a hefty price tag. The most expensive Wilardy model, the rhinestone treasure chest, sold for seventy-five dollars in 1956, more than a month's rent at that time. Popular with starlets, showgirls, and society dames, the Wilardy bag was the '50s equivalent of today's Dior Cadillac bag—not so much worn as paraded. With distinctly feminine handles that were designed to curve into the crook of the arm, each new model strove to be a show-stopper. "My shapes come from everywhere," says Will

*Sculptural bracelet bag, 1950*

Hardy. "I was inspired by thoughts of the future [rocket bags], by women's fashion [hatbox shaped bags]. And by Marilyn Monroe—all those curves!"

The success of the Wilardy bag pivoted on innovative geometric lines and radical shapes: ellipses, pyramids, tall arcing lids, and lollipop handles became Wilardy trademarks. The subtly undulating curved side of his lunch pail bag and the rounded compartments of his concertina box bag stacked together like a pile of books.

Awarded the first prize for accessories by the International Fashion Institute for his streamlined caramel box bag in 1954, Wilardy hired forty people for his New York factory and turned out over seventy models a day. His fortunes multiplied as swiftly as his copyists and the young designer spent much of the '50s litigating and protecting his patents. But the lifespan of Lucite as a luxury item was cut short by the invention of injection molding, a process that could make hard plastic bags cheaply and quickly. By 1958, cookie-cutter copies of Wilardy bags could be had for a fifth of the price, and his wealthy clientele moved on.

*Movie-star style, 1952–54*

*Prize winner, 1954*

Until the '90s, Wilardy's design legacy lay dormant. Stashed away in his own house, sold at flea markets, and generally deemed a curiosity of the atomic age, his bags floated outside of fashion like elegant space-junk. A return to '50s style, and Robert Gottlieb's book *A Certain Style: The Art of the Plastic Handbag, 1949–59,* brought them back. Today vintage Wilardy bags attract international collectors and once again are worn by movie stars and society girls, albeit with a certain ironic wink.

Chanel, Calvin Klein, and Helmut Lang have all released contemporary Lucite bags but none bear the eccentric extremes of the mid-century Wilardys. His originals were static and yet smoothly sensual, masculine and feminine, monumental and whimsically kitsch. The clarity of his lines and the dramatic angles of his handles and hardware took the handbag to a strange and sculptural place—a place where looks and luxury were meant to last forever.

*Signature swirl handle, 1955*

TENSION BETWEEN organic
ornament and geometric
form is a hallmark of a
Joyce Francis creation.
Fragile autumn leaves
swirl within the body
of her monumental
acrylic bag.

JOYCE FRANCIS,
2001

CARTOONS AND CUBISM inspired the witty figural bags of the Depression. Designed both to amuse and to function sleekly, the fan was a favorite form.

KORET, 1930s

CLASSICAL THEMES inspired the first handbags. Fashionably flat and shaped like a lyre, this design bridges the gap between the fragile silk reticule of 1800 and the sturdy travel bag that was to emerge later in the century.

AUSTRIAN, 1820

ALL SINGING, ALL DANCING, European high culture and Hollywood musical high jinks met in the novelty bags of Anne Marie of France. This mandolin-shaped bag came in a box decorated with an opera program.

ANNE MARIE OF FRANCE, 1930s

MASCULINE MATERIALS, FEMININE WILES. What possessed a girl to carry a metal picnic basket or a bag shaped like a high-rise compact? In an era when everything from bras to stiletto heels had a harder edge, handbags were embossed or woven of metal.

GINA, 1953–55

A FIXATION WITH DURABILITY made accessories more architectural in the '50s. The handbag became a house and unassailable avant-garde fortress in one.

AMERICAN, 1950S

CAPSULE STYLE turns
the handbag into a
space oddity, vacuum
formed and smoothly
indestructible.

CALVIN KLEIN, 1999

THE GEOMETRY OF MODERN
bags is a knowing art,
alluding to everything
from the formalist sculp-
ture of Donald Judd to
the soft assemblages
of Claes Oldenberg.

ENGLISH, 2001

INNOCENCE AND EXPERIENCE, lingerie and lipstick. The glamour of '50s style was created by suggestive contradictions. A rigid plastic bag rendered in sheer black lace is both formidable and inviting.

PATRICIA OF MIAMI, 1953

LITTLE RED RIDING HOOD goes to the cocktail lounge and orders a Bloody Mary. The deep folds of an evening purse are given a lascivious charm in scarlet patent leather.

SONIA RYKIEL, 2001

COVERT INTELLIGENCE
was the key to Cold War
glamour bags. Concealing
a mirror and compact
within its sleek, glittery
frame, this one is smarter
than it seems.

AMERICAN, 1950s

DECEPTIVELY SIMPLE, a bias-cut beaded pouch secrets a zip within its folds. Inspired by the sinuous evening gowns of Vionnet, structure is enveloped within organic form, with a simple looping button to hold it all together.

FRENCH, 1930s

PURISTS BE DAMNED, the fun of '50s bags is their bizarre couplings of bold geometric form and girlie trimmings.

WILARDY, 1956

THE INDU BAG BY LULU GUINNESS fuses art deco geometry and '50s frippery —a vintage cocktail of style and silhouette.

LULU GUINNESS, 1999

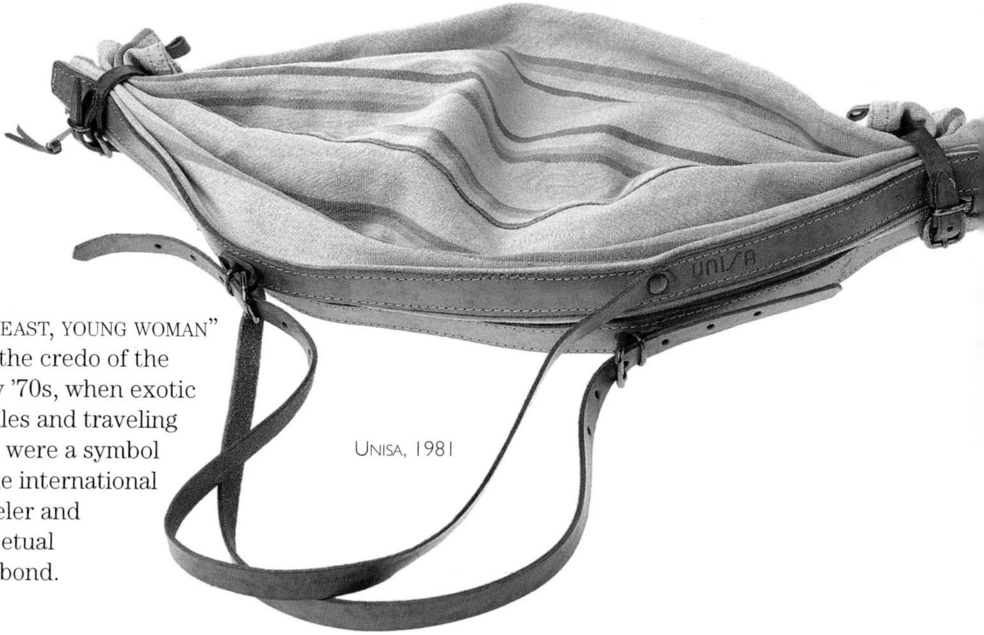

"GO EAST, YOUNG WOMAN"
was the credo of the
early '70s, when exotic
textiles and traveling
bags were a symbol
of the international
traveler and
perpetual
vagabond.

UNISA, 1981

BOXY PURSES AND POCHETTES died out in the early '70s because they represented formality and structure. As clothes loosened, so did handbags. Ethnic bags from Asia and South America not only provided an emblem of adventure, but also exploded the notion that a bag had to be a box with straps.

CENTRAL AMERICAN, 1970S

A PASSION FOR THE SQUARE
has held Hermès in good
stead since the 1920s.
Smooth and solid as
an office block shape,
this box bag features
no external hardware
and may be opened
by pressing the subtle
button hidden beneath
its skin.

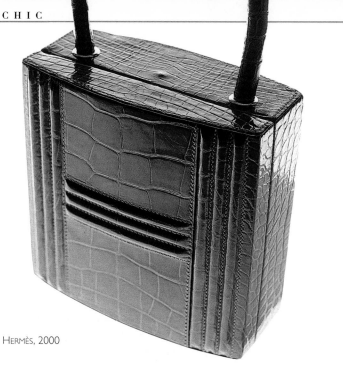

HERMÈS, 2000

CRISP, COOL, AND COLLECTED—that is the impact of a bag with a strong silhouette. Walter Steiger brings couture tailoring to a trim little day bag, creating the illusion of a collar and bow tie in one.

WALTER STEIGER, 2001

PIERRE BALMAIN LOVED the locket; he featured lockets as necklaces season after season and then he immortalized one in the elegant ellipse of a suede cocktail bag.

PIERRE BALMAIN, 1940s

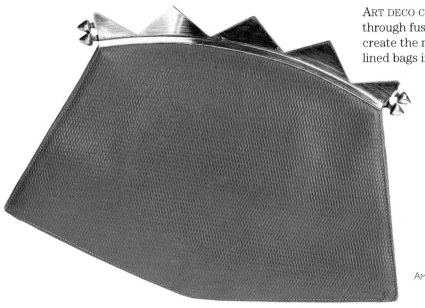

ART DECO CUT A SWATH
through fuss and frills to
create the most stream-
lined bags in history.

AMERICAN, 1930s

MODERNISM HAS BEEN A DANCE between the oval and the square. Framed in gold, Emilio Pucci's sculpted bag takes on the look of an art print. Graphic, groovy, and good to go.

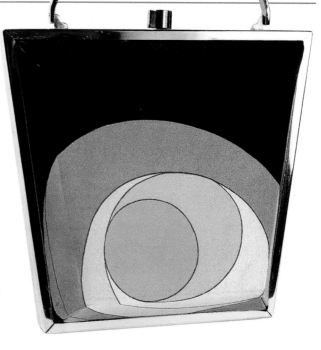

PUCCI, 1969

THE PRINCE OF PATTERN, Emilio Pucci excelled in creating luxury from unpretentious materials and fabulous prints. This velveteen bag structured with card has a solid metal clasp that doubles as a frame. Designed to swing, no doubt, from a long and deeply suntanned arm.

PUCCI, MID-1960s

Organic forms take us back to nature, evoking the skins and tendrils that probably hung from the most ancient hunting bags. In the 15th century, bags were ruched together into deeply folded pockets, first with drawstrings and then mounted onto metal frames.

German money purses, 15th century

THE PASSION FOR POM-POMS, leather fringe, and intricate knots was revived in the late '60s and early '70s, when shapes and materials softened and the bag became radically deconstructed.

CARLOS FALCHI MACRAMÉ BAG, 1970

# CARLOS FALCHI: ON THE FRINGE

**B**orn in Minas Gerias, Brazil, Carlos Falchi made his first handbags at the age of six for his cousin, and his aunts loved them. In 1969 he worked nights at Max's Kansas City, the infamous Manhattan bar, in a pair of homemade snakeskin patchwork pants, and Miles Davis loved them. In 1974 he designed the squashy soft leather Buffalo duffel bag, and women everywhere loved them: He won a Coty Award in 1983 and inspired squads of copyists.

Relaxed, expansive, and romantic, Falchi still works with raw-edged leathers, macramé knots, and acid-rock colors, but his bags have evolved way beyond his simple supple pouches of the

**"I want to be able to squash and trash a bag and still see it keep going."**
*— Falchi*

*Signature satchels, 1980s*

*Carlos Falchi's rock-and-roll handbag empire began unexpectedly after he encased Mick Jagger's bottom in patchwork leather.*

'70s. Today, classic snakeskin day bags, crystal-studded pochettes, and sporty leather-trimmed canvas totes balance out Falchi's wilder excesses, luring back the sort of client that might shy away from lime-green snakeskin with knee-length '60s fringe.

"By not being a handbag maker," says Falchi, "I broke the rules of handbag making. I made vessels, things for carrying your stuff around." These "vessels" appealed to the likes of Mick Jagger, Tina Turner, and Herbie Hancock's wife, who told the designer, "Go to Bendel's." When Falchi trucked up to the department store with a tote full of bags, skins, scissors, and tools, the buyer, Jerry Stutz, saw the tiny medieval-style coin bag around his neck and sent him home to stitch up some more. "You know, bags were very stiff in the '60s, more like weapons than accessories," says Falchi.

*Fringe bags, 2000–2002*

"I would take my leathers and dye them in the bathtub at home using crazy Analine colors. Nothing matched and they were very light[weight]. At a time when everyone was crying out for freedom, I made bags that swung, that moved and caressed the body."

In the late '70s, Falchi made collage pochettes in metallic snakeskin, dramatic, bullet-shaped, tiny necklace-sized disco bags, and loopy white leather knotted shoulder bags that looked like ragged feathers. Malleable and soft, Falchi's bags traveled well and suited the generation who lived in frayed jeans and cowboy boots. Moving into the punk era, the designer modeled fur satchels on Mohawk hairdos and streaked luxury leathers like alligator with wild smears of acid-yellow and Day-Glo pink. The deceptively simple

*The Heraldic, early 1980s*

*The Octagon, late 1970s*

*Harlequin bag, 1989*

shapes of his best bags—the organic drawstring folds of the "signature" bag and the vast ruched arc of his leather shoulder bag—were imitated and mass produced globally.

Despite his self-styled rebel image, Falchi continued to make sophisticated evening bags throughout the '80s and '90s, improvising with sculptural form. His folding box bag with a central opening of interlocking leather petals was based on a Florentine coin purse, his hexagonal tricolor tricorn bag for Todd Oldham was inspired by a harlequin's cap. Falchi's contribution to sculptural form was to literally turn the bag inside out, making a leather shoulder bag look like a wonton, a bat's wing, or an unfurling petal with a fringe of loose stems. After thirty years, the designer remains adamant about keeping his bags soft and sexy. "This," he says, squeezing a big chunk of hairy calfskin, "is all caveman stuff. It's primal!"

*Patchwork 'Kelly', 1980s*

ZIPPY DIAGONALS,
swooping curves,
and arcing, looped
circles. This was the
geometric legacy of
a decade of deco style.

GERMAN, 1936–39

"Everything in your closet
should have an expiration
date on it the way milk and
bread and magazines do."
—*Andy Warhol*

BUILT FOR COMFORT, STYLED FOR SPEED. John Galliano gets behind the wheel of an entirely new handbag concept with his Trailer bag for Christian Dior, equipped with headlights, a license plate, and perforated "upholstery" leather.

CHRISTIAN DIOR, 2001

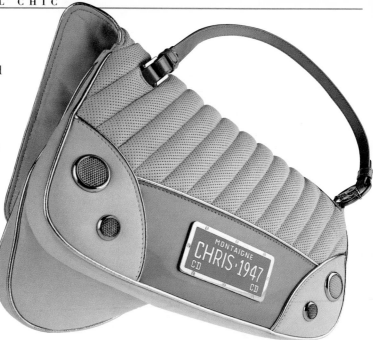

THE FOCI BAG by the Brooklyn-based design firm Ply takes the classic '50s bucket shape and updates it, creating a delicate play between positive and negative space with a cutout handle.

PLY, 2001

A BEADED LANTERN BAG
of the 1900s echoed the
handkerchief hem of tea-
dance gowns. It floats
at the wrist and folds
perfectly flat.

FRENCH, c. 1905

NOTHING STRUTS ITS SHAPE
like the clutch, the bag
designed for blatantly
theatrical decoration.

NATORI, 2002

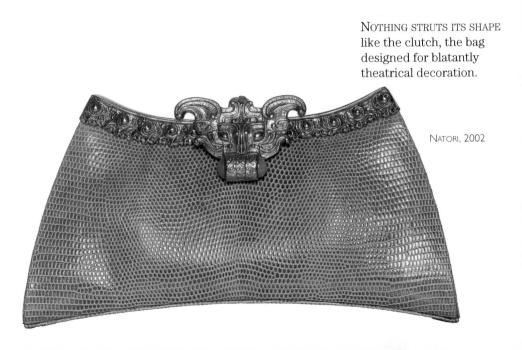

INDUSTRIAL DESIGN AND
DELICATE DETAILS meet
in a sophisticated bag of
chrome frame, Bakelite
handle, and molded
leather rosebuds.

FRENCH, 1930

AS ELABORATE
AS A PIRATE CHEST,
this molded leather
bag packs monumental
scale into its petite
proportions.

GERMAN, 1850

FORM FOLLOWS FUNCTION in a travel bag that holds its own stationery drawer. Designed for train travel, this personal portmanteau was the first portable office.

GERMAN, 1905

GAS-MASK HANDBAGS were designed by the British government in World War II to resemble everyday bags—sturdy, sensible, thrifty, and safe.

BRITISH, 1940

# BAGS AND THE BODY

There is something stiffly self conscious about carrying a structured handbag with a little top handle. Like the affectation of gloves or a fan, the gesture of carrying a bag at a dainty distance from the body deems it ladylike by virtue of its old-fashioned discomfort.

Shoulder bags and backpacks were, for most of history, worn only by peasants and revolutionaries. (Perhaps this is why they've always been the favorite bag of the avant-garde.) A bag wedded to the body invites radical design experiments. Issey Miyake used pleated nylon for a delicate backpack that expands and contracts like a little wing on the shoulder blade.

Yohji Yamamoto's idea to suspend a large, beaded sequin evening bag from the back of a long black dress exploded the notion that the backpack was androgynous or antifashion. But despite the rare attempt to make a

*Michael Kors, 2002*

backpack or fanny pack feminine, the vision of a bag as integral to clothing rather than a separate accessory is almost always sporty and unisex. Materials usually associated with surfing and hiking—microfiber, Velcro, and neoprene—have made body bags more sculptural and futuristic. Like the elaborate mutations of contemporary running shoes, Miu Miu's back packs and messenger totes of 1999 made extravagant use of nylon mesh, vinyl, and active-wear fabrics, making the laziest girl look purposeful.

*Jean Charles de Castelbajac, 1999*

*Miu Miu, 1999*

Jean Charles de Castelbajac turned the bag into a physical environment, making bag-coats with dozens of pouched compartments, or bubble bags, sewn directly onto the jackets. "When I design, I construct like a builder," says Castelbajac. "The body is the room and the pockets are the closets."

The passion for utility bag fashions worn snug to the body seems to be the natural outcome of life in big cities. Handbags are not built for speed, but a messenger bag, worn slung from hip to shoulder and smothered in handy zippers, suits the bus or subway dash to the office. Bags worn on the body also take a defensive stance; the fantasy of Dior's new Street Chic wrist bags is that of the fashionista guerrilla. The bags, worn bracelet-style, feature the multiple pockets of grenade belts

*Jean Charles de Castelbajac, 2000;*
*Right: Dooney and Bourke, 2000*

*Michael Kors, 2001*

and the heavy canvas straps of old army bags. Body bags can also serve as comfort: A gigantic shoulder bag can be a surrogate home, and a bag sewn directly onto your clothes adopts an almost anatomical intimacy. Less contrived, more masculine, and always more modern than the bag-as-object, the bag that joins the body is no longer an external appendage or an affectation of style. It is, instead, truly a part of you.

*Prada messenger-style bags, 1999*

ISSEY MIYAKE'S "spiral bag" is based on the blazing red bustier he designed for Grace Jones, the reigning glamazon of '80s fashion.

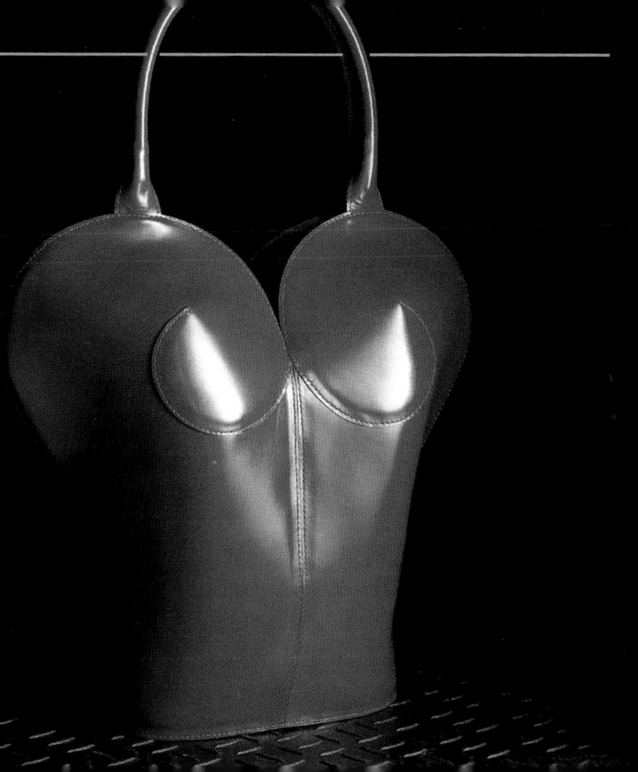

ISSEY MIYAKE, 1991

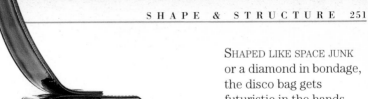

SHAPED LIKE SPACE JUNK or a diamond in bondage, the disco bag gets futuristic in the hands of Thierry Mugler.

THIERRY MUGLER, 1980s

MILLENNIUM HANDBAGS THINK outside the square, with curvy handles and bulging bellies. Could this be the design decade of the doughnut?

BORBONESSE, 2001

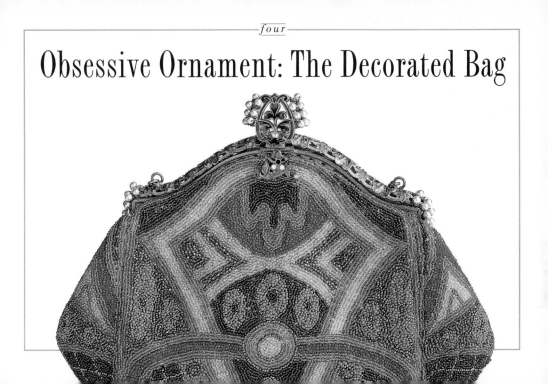

# four

# Obsessive Ornament: The Decorated Bag

Embroidered, beaded, ruffled, bejeweled, and feathered, bags have belonged to the richest women and to the most inventive. Mary, Queen of Scots, whiled away her days in the Tower of London embroidering bags as gifts to her captors, a skill passed down to her from Catherine de Medici. In her era, ornament adorned both sexes; men carried tasseled, opulent coin purses and wallets emblazoned with heraldic symbols. Like lace, which cost more than gold in the 15th century, the bespoke bag belonged to kings, queens, and priests, an expression of the privilege of possessing money, rare

*Polish, 18th century; Above right: Elizabethan sweet purse, 16th century; Previous page: Czechoslovakian, 1920s*

documents, sachets of exotic scent, or imported tobacco. Cut from rare cloths, studded with gems, or simply labored over by unnamed artisans, the first "power bags" used trim to set their owner apart. Decorative bags were also used as messengers in the game of courtly love, conveying an intimate missive in the language of flowers or embroidered poesy. This idea of carrying your heart on your wrist instead of your sleeve lends the decorative bag a flirtatious appeal that more sensible designs lacked.

The urge to festoon a bag is an ancient one that has withstood sumptuary laws, politics, and war. When Marie Antoinette was beheaded, all of her frilly accoutrements rolled with her. After the French revolution, rococo fripperies were deemed immoral by the state. Just as the philosopher Jean-Jacques Rousseau rejected

*French wallet, 18th century*

"flowery language" for plain speech, Paris fashion rejected flowery trims and fussiness on everything from dress to accessories. After decades of bags shaped like Grecian urns and droopy tulips, the romantics and then the Victorians brought back ornament and fancy trims. The rising merchant classes wanted to show off their wealth and, not unlike in our own times, they used the handbag to do it. Clasps wrought from solid silver, mock medieval chatelaines, beads of jet, Venetian glass, and cut steel heavily encrusted the bag a lady took to tea or to the opera.

*German, 1860*

In the Victorian era, for every bag created by artisans and sold in stores that specialized in "fantasie," bibelot, and luggage, there were thousands being stitched at home. Magazines such as *Godey's Lady's Book* provided patterns for elaborate embroidery, and strange receptacles (somewhere between box and bag) were fashioned of card, glue, ribbon, and velvet. The Victorian urge to smother every surface with pattern led to bizarre bags: money wallets trimmed with papal ribbons, and silken purses with hand-painted scenes of Gothic ruins and maudlin widows. Pattern books also kept the American sampler tradition alive, producing bags that borrowed from the beadwork of the Native Americans, with rigid little houses floating against bright blue skies. The sentimentality and regimentation of such designs reflected a strangely static ideal of home and hearth, but as women moved into the world their bags went with them, picking up all manner of exotic influence and flights of fancy along the way.

There were so many kinds of decorated bags at the start of the new century that it

*French, 1900s*

is impossible to identify a definitive style. Most opulent were the beaded bags imported from France, Germany, and Czechoslovakia. Based on Persian carpets, art nouveau gardens, and lush abstractions, these bags brought sophistication to those who could afford them as well as a decidedly decadent sensibility. It seems that fashion turns to fantasy when reality is too confrontational or change too radical.

During World War I, romantic dress was at its height and bags were never more delicate, adorned with antique lace and cabbage roses. Even during the Depression, when the handbag shrunk in size, there was a taste for Shakespearean ruched velvets and decorative jeweled clasps. Bending to social trends, ornament on bags grew femininely

*Above, and detail:*
*Bohemian beaded*
*bag, 1910*

*CC=Conspicuous Consumption, Crazy Chic, and Coco Chanel*

floral in the '50s, militant in the late '60s with chunky buckles and hardware, and funky and folkloric in the '70s.

The tradition of a family crest ennobling the front of a bag as a status symbol was revived in the '80s by the aggressive initials of designer logos. The gigantic interlocking Cs cast in gold on the front of a Chanel bag inspired many designers to up the ante and make their names the predominant feature of a bag. Who wanted polka dots or pinstripes when you could have STATUS writ large across your shoulder? The Fendi baguette took that '80s spirit of excess and updated it for the late '90s. The success and fame of the baguette was not based on its shape—such a plain little envelope— but on its crazy and wildly entertaining trimmings.

*Fendi, 2001*

Cut from embroidered damask, Indian mirrored cotton, snakeskin, satin, and suede, each limited-edition bag combined elitism with folk charm. The constantly changing models fed our addictive lust for bags as sequels and second acts, and it came to pass that the decorative bag became a very expensive baseball card for grown-ups: collected, discussed, known for every minute change to their design, color, and form.

Such a passion is understandable. As clothing has become more and more minimal, ornament no longer adorns the entire body. The desire for plumage, be it clumps of sequins or macramé knots, gravitates to the bag when it has nowhere else to go. Today, the handbag seems the last place for theater in fashion. Christian Lacroix mounts a starburst

*Christian Dior, 2001*

*Bottega Veneta, 2001*

of faux jewels on a bag of torn metallic leather like a broken tiara for a punk princess. Marni, a recent cult design house in Milan, takes a fistful of diamond bracelets, brooches, and chokers and winds them around the strap of a butch leather bag studded with bronze, then adds a foxtail and a silk rose for good measure. Each new hyperdecorative bag on the block attempts to out-glitz the last or makes a self-referential joke about the bags of the season before. Now that there are bags *about* bags, the spirit of ornament is heady but far from innocent. The power of a lavish modern bag is not just its luxury materials but the insider knowledge implied by its design. A rose, scented with irony and handbag history, is no longer just a rose.

*Marni, 2002*

THE MODERN WEDDING BAG is often the most ornamental purse a woman will ever own, and the most old-fashioned. The tradition of the purse as medieval symbol of female chattel and worldly wealth is revisited in a lacy pouch adorned with a vintage clasp shaped like a cupola.

REVIVALS, 1999

ORNAMENT AS A STATUS INDICATOR can be positively heavy-handed, especially in medieval design, which spelled out the worldly wealth of the owner in aggressive terms. This early cut-velvet bag may have been used for hunting on the castle grounds.

FRENCH, 15TH CENTURY

THE ELIZABETHANS LOVED their pom-poms, bedecking sweet bags and purses with elaborate fringe and woven baubles. French designers Jamin Puech have a passion for historical detail and update the courtly tradition in crocheted Lurex yarn.

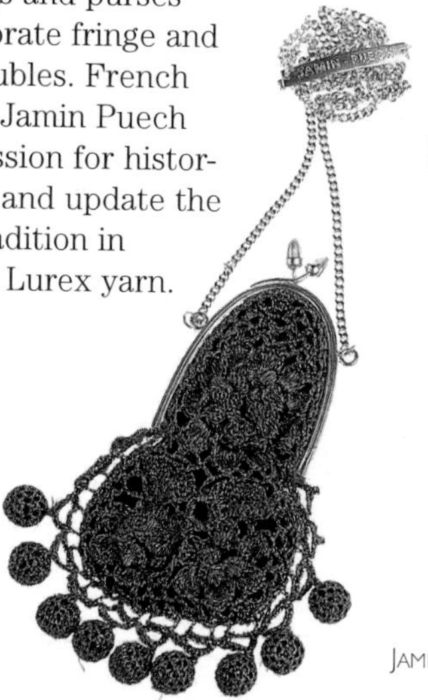

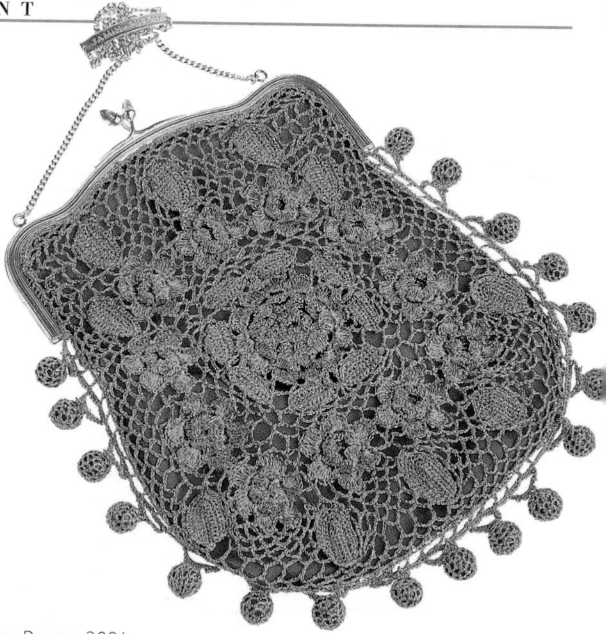

JAMIN PUECH, 2001

A MAN'S PURSE was a fashionable accessory in the 16th century, worn suspended from a belt along with daggers and swords, and made more potent with detailed ornament. The gilded brass goblins on this one make an aggressively stylish statement.

ENGLISH, 1550

IN 18TH-CENTURY AMERICA, Irish stitch was worked on costly imported linen into a vibrant durable cloth that covered chairs, wallets, and ladies' pockets.

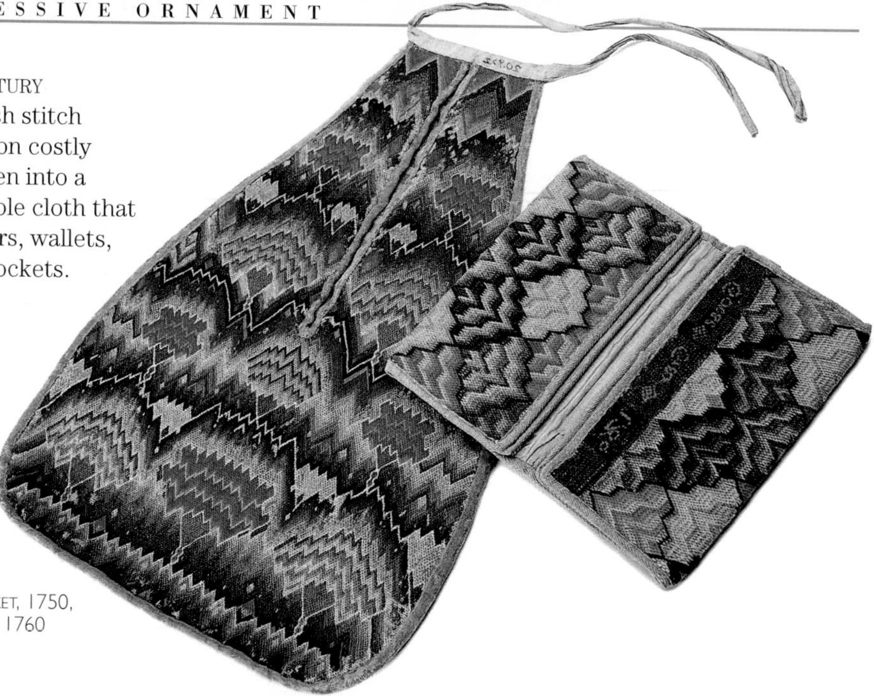

LADY'S LARGE POCKET, 1750, AND POCKETBOOK, 1760

LONG BEFORE THE TOTE, 18th-century ladies wore long pockets laced about their waists. Secreted beneath petticoats and hooped skirts, they ported knitting patterns, poems, prayer books, and ribbons. So treasured were the contents that women were known to bequeath their pockets in their wills.

AMERICAN, 1780s

JANE AUSTEN WAS HANDY WITH A NEEDLE, making several little bags for members of her family and often embroidering them with her own witticisms. This bag came from the estate of her brother Edward Austen Knight—whether it was one of Jane's remains a mystery.

ENGLISH, 1790S

A VOLUMINOUS SILKEN BODY and sculpted base were characteristic of the 18th-century work bag or "knotting" bag, resembling something between a petticoat and bishop's hat.

GERMAN WORK BAG, EARLY 1800s

INSTEAD OF LOGOS, heraldic symbols and family crests adorned the bags of the 15th and 16th centuries, announcing the court and title of the owner. On this purse the crests are hand painted—unusual in an age of rich embroidery.

GERMAN, 1586

POWER BAGS don't come more blatant than this. Napoleon's "handbag" was designed for carrying official documents and letters. Napoleon commissioned a series of these deep-green, gold-embossed bags for his entourage, including his sister Pauline, who used hers, it is said, to carry love letters.

FRENCH, 1810

HANDBAG ORNAMENT
is not always girlishly
fey. This revolutionary
reticule from France
features delicate flowers
on one side and a
brazenly political blue
"Liberté" cap on the
other. *Vive le sac!*

FRENCH, 1790s

TODAY THERE ARE MESSAGE T-SHIRTS; in the early 19th century there was the message handbag. This silk reticule was used to carry pamphlets on emancipation and may have been sold to raise funds for the Ladies Society for the Relief of Negro Slaves, founded in England in 1725.

ENGLISH, 1827

WHEN REVOLUTION AND WAR LEFT France poor at the end of the 18th century, cut-steel beads replaced precious stones as a popular ornament. In the 19th century these beads flourished on miser's purses, rounded reticules, and wrist bags. This trio of Victorian bags still glitters with electroplated cut-steel beads.

BRITISH, 1850s–60s

THE MUTED COLORS of pale gray and silver enjoyed a revival in the early '30s when fashion magazines fancied all things Grecian, from columns to neoclassical Wedgwood cameos.

AMERICAN, EARLY 1930S

"He who would travel
happily must travel light."
—*Antoine de Saint-Exupery*

THE FIRST LITHOGRAPHS ever applied to a bag were from Offenbach, the German city where Mozart's music was printed. This rare box bag is decorated with scenes of the barracks and city hall in Frankfurt.

GERMAN, 1830

Year-long honeymoons in Europe were not uncommon for wealthy Victorians. Opulent souvenir bags completed the journey. Some were made of hand-colored lithographs of Paris in fancy gilded mounts. One gold-plated box bag (far right) had the Pont-Neuf, the Place de la Concorde, and the Église Trinité hand painted onto its decorative panels.

French souvenir reticule, 1855

FRENCH BOX BAG, 1860

WHAT WERE THE VICTORIANS THINKING? Mid-19th-century crocheted miser's pouch purses hung like exotic sea slugs from the belts of prudent housewives, after the medieval custom of carrying coins in a sock. Men wore them too, but theirs were up to three times longer, stuffed into coat pockets or unfurled like a fob chain. A tiny hidden slit at the bag's center released its contents very slowly, hence the name.

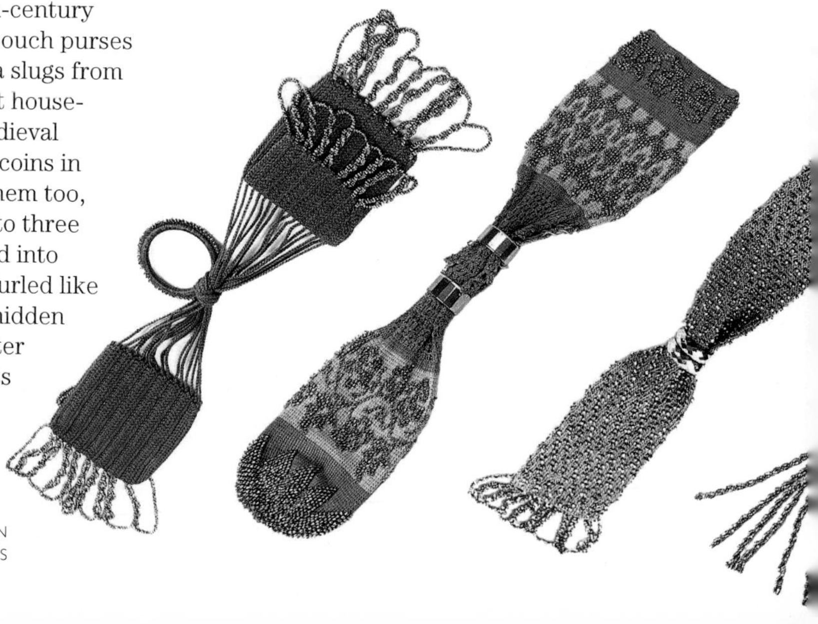

BRITISH AND AMERICAN
MISER BAGS, 1840s–60s

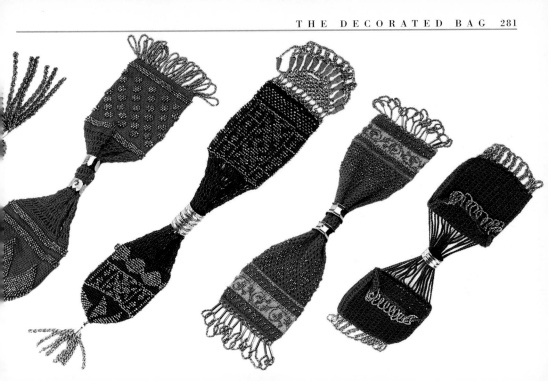

ECCENTRICITY WAS THE hallmark of handmade bags based on the patterns and craft magazines women cherished right up to World War I. Pink satin, upholstery trim, ribbon, and card are the sugary stuff of a strange creation, hand painted with an Italianate glaze and with little satin balls for feet.

AMERICAN, 1900s

THE LANGUAGE OF ORNAMENT can be cryptic. On one side of a funeral purse sits a country squire and on the other a pining woman at a spinning wheel. Separated by death, or merely two sides of the same bag?

AMERICAN, 1870

VICTORIANS DEEMED it proper to grieve for up to three years in shades of black, violet, and blue. These funeral bags in hand-beaded velvet and Venetian beads made mourning modish.

ENGLISH, 1860s

"LOVE IS VIRTUE'S REWARD," moralizes this handmade beaded bag.

GERMAN, EARLY 19TH CENTURY

THE AMERICAN ART
of weaving apple seeds
began in colonial times,
a humble craft that
yielded surprisingly
sophisticated little
bags with tiny interiors.
This one is unusual
for its blue silk lining
and its shape as an
evening reticule from
far fancier shores.

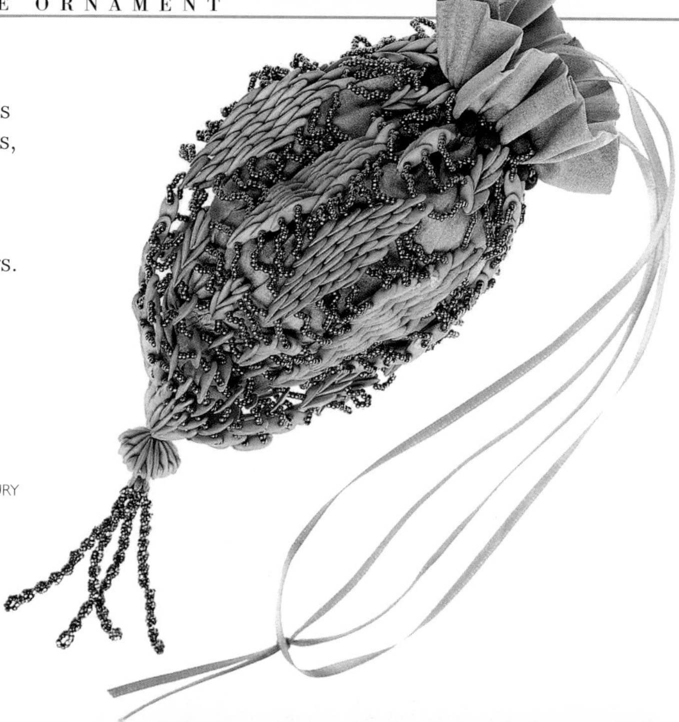

AMERICAN, EARLY 19TH CENTURY

THE FRENCH DESIGN DUO Jamin Puech adorned their Blixen bag with wooden rods carved to looked like bone, tiny macramé knots, matte sequins, and a long swinging fringe. The result is a dance bag that sings.

JAMIN PUECH, 2000

## JAMIN PUECH: THE DREAM TEAM

From the age of seven to the age of nineteen, Isabelle Puech lived on a sailboat, exploring the world by sea with her parents. Perhaps that is why her bags are ornamented with faded postcards, exotic embroidered foliage, and a rich palette of muted tropical color. Created with her husband, Benoit Jamin, a Jamin Puech bag connotes nostalgia, patina, sensuality, and exploration. These bags seem to be from the era before airplane travel: leathers smoked by railway carriages and evening bags that swung in the breeze of the top deck. Who else would name a handbag collection "Travels and life of a tattooed sailor"? Jamin Puech hoards raffia from Madagascar, coconut buttons from Polynesia, silk from Vietnam,

*Journeys are a recurring theme for a designer who grew up on a yacht. Coin purse, 2001; Above: Tahiti bag, 1995*

*Wed to their work, design duo Benoit Jamin and Isabelle Puech*

and great skeins of antique ribbon from Lyon; their Paris atelier looks like a cross between Gauguin's studio and a Belle Époque hat shop. It is certainly a world away from the marketing meetings, handbag focus groups, and technical research labs of the billion-dollar design houses. Having started small in 1988, the design duo like to keep a sense of eccentricity and tactility in every bag they create. Sourcing the knitting, weaving, and hand beading for each bag out to small cottage workshops across France, Jamin Puech limit their collections to fifty thousand bags a year—modest in comparison to the large houses, but still a significant leap from their first collection, which was created on a kitchen table in a small Parisian apartment.

*Purple walls and silken cushions adorn the jewel-like Jamin Puech boutique in Paris.*

*From the boudoir collection, 1988–89*

Fresh from studying costume design in Paris in the late '80s, the couple turned to making bags as an extension of their couture skills. "Our desire in the beginning," Isabelle says, "was to put all of the fabrics and techniques of costume into the bag." Their first collection was a sugary affair of quilted boudoir satins and marabou powder-puff evening bags. In tune with the surrealist revival in French couture, these bags provided a coquettish antidote to the buffed leather briefcases and trim little backpacks of the late '80s.

The collections that followed played with millinery straw, plastics, bronzed leathers, and hand-painted canvas, but the bags that made Jamin Puech a cult favorite were hand beaded and embroidered. Onto simple square totes and rectangular evening pouches lined in silk, the couple sewed matte sequins, broad embroidery stitches, patchwork,

*Beaded palette bag, 1999*

and fringe in distinctly old-world colors. The combination of the folksy handwork and a sophisticated palette struck just the right chord with women who had rejected the aggressive logos of '80s handbags and were searching for a softer, less corporate image. Models like Helena Christensen and Kate Moss adopted the Jamin Puech evening bag, wearing them with low-slung jeans and sheer '30s-style dresses. Arriving three or four years before the Fendi baguette, these delicate designs brought sensual texture and intimate scale back to the bag. Featuring striking but subtle contrasts between tulle and metallic leathers, dull bronze rivets and matte sequins, satin and fur, the Jamin Puech bag was the bohemian alternative to the sensible early-'90s day bag.

*Gum leaf bag, 1999*

*Sequin bag, 2001*

"There is no special recipe to the creation of a bag collection; it comes by feeling, by desire, and sometimes the story emerges after a collection is finished."

—*Isabelle Puech*

*Mother and baby matte sequins, 1988*

Subsequent seasons drew inspiration from Bloomsbury, Tahiti, Agatha Christie's *Murder on the Orient Express,* Edwardian patchwork, and the Wild West. Uniting these disparate themes is Isabelle and Benoit's use of color. Researched through constant travel, flea market trawls, and regular trips to European museums, Jamin Puech bags possess extraordinary tonal range. They can evoke the sulfurous glow of the Nabi painters—acrid yellow with dove gray, lilac with chocolate, mint green and magenta—or the ripe, bleeding fruits of a Bonnard still life. To get the contrasts right, Isabelle and Benoit make countless watercolor studies. Each collection features eighty-two designs in a minimum of five color schemes.

*Patchwork, 2000*

The results are bags that look as if they belong on the arm of Madame Matisse. "It's hard to make a mistake with black," says Isabelle. "It's the easy way out, and that is probably why we avoid it."

Moving into embossed leathers, structured bags, and more traditional hardware, the Jamin Puech style has refined itself over the past decade. The simple pocket shape of the early bags has evolved into curvy-bottomed carpetbags and sophisticated day bags; their trademark thin leather straps have branched into sculpted plastic handles and necklace chains. The company once devoted to satin and silk tulle now works with exotic leathers, canvas seriographed with photography, and straw. Seasonally hailed as the accessory for true romantics, Jamin Puech bags appeal to restless spirits, women who see why snakeskin and newsprint are a perfect match and are more than happy to wear their sequins in broad daylight.

*Organza and silk ribbon, 2002*

MILKMAIDS, FAIRY-TALE CASTLES, and shady coves are the stuff of chocolate box art and the very costly "scenery" bags of the 1910s and '20s. The favorite subject of the Italian bags were gondolas and proto-Renaissance landscapes, and for the Germans, Neuschwanstein Castle, the turreted folly built by Mad King Ludwig II between 1869 and 1886.

GERMAN, 1900s

GERMAN, FRENCH, AND ITALIAN VENETIAN-
BEADED BAGS, C. MID-19TH CENTURY

THE GLASS BEAD was born as a tiny molten blob in Venice in the 13th century. Venetian beads were known for their pure color, tiny size, and painstaking production. Bohemian beads, made in Czechoslovakia from the early 1800s to the 1920s, were larger and slightly coarser, and they faded over time.

AUSTRIAN BEADED
RETICULE, C. 1910

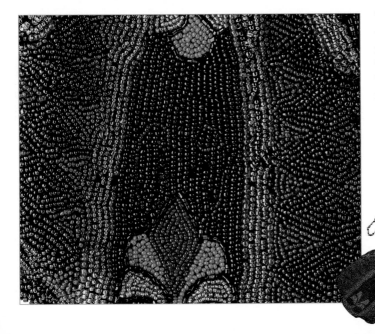

VIEWING THE TWO BAGS up close, we see the major difference between the two breeds of bead: The Venetian (far left) is meticulously tiny and slightly iridescent, the Bohemian chunky and overtly sensual. Bold geometric patterns rather than ornate flowers suited the Bohemian bead.

BOHEMIAN EVENING BAG, 1920s

"WITH THIS BAG I THEE WED."
Presented to the bride
to prove the bounty of
her groom during the
wedding ceremony, these
silk purses adorned with
cameo portraits on each
side were created by
Limoges in the late
17th century.

LIMOGES, C. 1690s

BY THE 20TH CENTURY the cameo had become merely a decorative feature, ornamenting a velvet opera bag with purely imaginary noble pretensions.

EUROPEAN, C. 1900

THE WEDDING BAG, pretty and adorned with petite point, beads, or velvet flowers, is fast becoming a fashionable stand-in for the bridal bouquet.

PONT ST. BEAUVAIS, 1950s

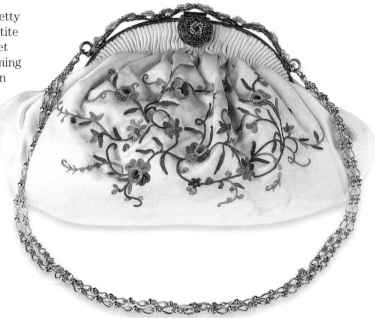

BELGIAN, FOR NEIMAN MARCUS, 1950s

JUDITH LEIBER, 2002

For her wedding day, Mindy Spencer, half of the Australian design team of Spencer and Rutherford, went all out, creating an embroidered, fringed, and bespangled wrist bag worthy of the Sun King.

SPENCER AND RUTHERFORD, 2000

"All things feminine and beautiful with a touch of wit are what I love in a bag."
—*Lulu Guinness*

LULU GUINNESS WEDDING BAG, 1999

A MAGIC CARPET RIDE created an exotic
illusion and the perfect pattern for
a hexagonal beaded bag. Here three
different designs adopt the rug in
evolving mutations from the opulent
to the abstract.

BOHEMIAN, 1900–10

ITALIAN BEADED BAG,
c. 1910

AUSTRIAN BEADED POCHETTE, c. 1925–29

Cubism made it hip to
be square. Machines,
skyscrapers, and pure
abstract form were the
streamlined motifs of
modernist design.

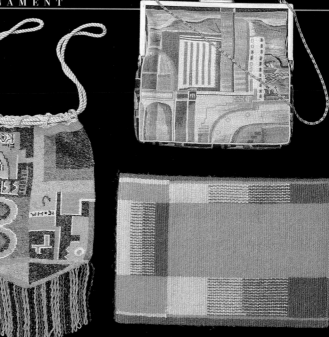

Weiner Werkstadt art
deco bags, 1920–30

THE GREAT COLONIAL EXPOSITION of Paris opened in 1922, bringing African art to artists and designers. Tutankhamen's tomb was discovered the same year, generating a renewed exoticism in design.

FRENCH, 1925

THE COMPLEX LANGUAGE OF FLOWERS so beloved by the Victorians was simplified in the 20th century. An innocent wrist bag in the shape of a pansy meant little more than the freedom to dance.

BELGIAN, 1920s

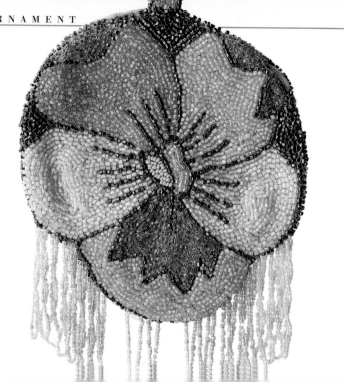

SHEER CLOTHING always brings bags back into proportion with the body. The sheath dresses and spaghetti-strapped slips of the '90s found their perfect match in the sinuous beaded bags of Jamin Puech.

JAMIN PUECH, 2001

BEFORE PAUL POIRET and Coco Chanel invented sportswear, exotic fantasy ruled fashion, and dance bags were richly festooned to match the last gasp of Belle Époque style. Smothered with antique lace and twisted ribbon roses, a dance bag matched the ruffled hems and Spanish shawls of the day.

AMERICAN, 1914

HYPERFEMININITY went out the window when hems went up and women went to work. The metal mesh bag of the '20s flapper streamlined ornament down to a shimmering skin and a silvery clasp.

WHITING AND DAVIS, 1920s

PAINTER RAOUL DUFY
didn't always work on
canvas. From 1912 to
1928 he created densely
colored and subtly optical
textile designs for the
French firm Bianchini
Férier. His brocade for
this bag depicts a day
at the races as pictured
in a tropical jungle—
colonial chic.

FRENCH, EARLY 1930S

TURKISH ORNAMENT influenced fashion from the 16th century through the Crimean War, infusing European purses, wallets, and reticules with rich gold and silver embroidery.

TURKISH, 1780–1810

VISIONS OF THE NATURAL WORLD change according to the taste of the times. For the designers of the Wiener Werkstadt, such as Josef Hoffman, a flower could be reduced to its abstract essence.

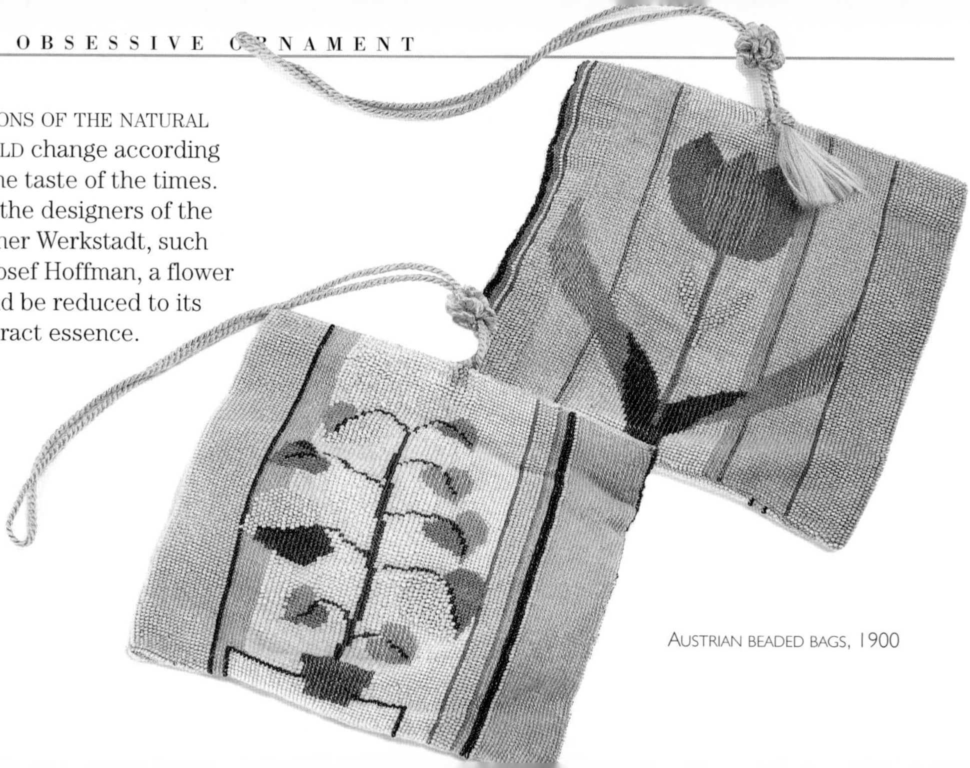

AUSTRIAN BEADED BAGS, 1900

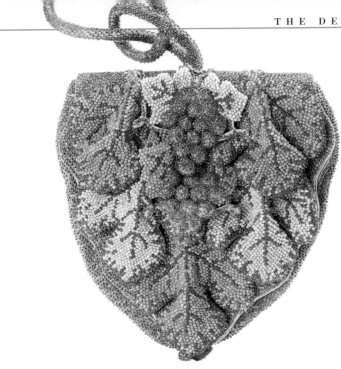

To the surrealists
a more baroque vision
of nature prevailed,
creating bags that
harked back to the
theatricality of the
18th century for their
sensual charge.

Marie Art Studio,
Shanghai, 1936

"A bag that's chic is a bag that you can wear everywhere, day or night. It has a sense of humour, a sort of tenderness."
—*Sonia Rykiel*

FRENCH, 19TH-CENTURY REVIVAL, 1920

THE INRO BAG,
by British designer
Nathalie Hambro,
is wrought from
embossed metal
sheeting and stainless-
steel gauze with a
cord of dulled silver.
"It is not only a fashion
accessory," Hambro says,
"but an objet d'art."

NATHALIE HAMBRO, 1993

IF THE BAG IS TO MATCH THE SHOE, these Chinese silk coin purses from the 19th century are in suitably shrunken proportion. Tiny lotus slippers matched delicate little bags that hung from a beaded silk cord, reinstating a powerfully restrained notion of feminine grace.

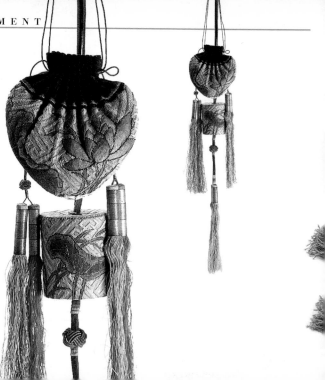

CHINESE COIN PURSES,
MID-19TH CENTURY

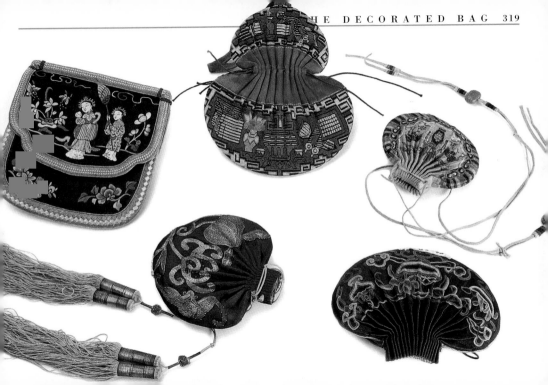

A FASCINATION FOR CHINOISERIE in the '20s brought a new wave of Chinese embroidery and modern materials applied in extraordinary ways: celluloid cast as ivory, raffia and ribbon wrought in stitches that resembled Fauvist brushstrokes. The most elaborate of this trio of '20s bags has silk appliqué, and chenille and velvet embroidery depicting elephants on one side and a leopard on the other.

FRENCH, 1920s–30s

MANY MODERN DESIGNERS turn to India for artisan beading, stitchwork, and even the casting of their hardware. English designer Megan Park's original watercolor design was executed in raffia at an Indian workshop.

MEGAN PARK, 2001

A WOMAN'S WORK BECAME her decoration, too, when the Victorian lady took to parading her trinkets from a chatelaine.

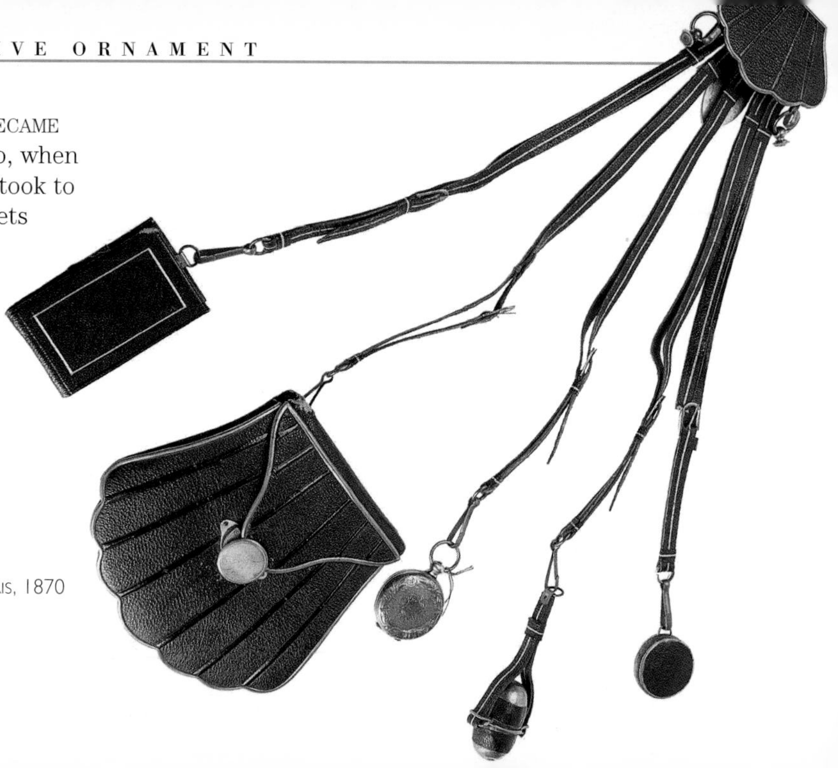

GALLARET OF PARIS, 1870

GOLDPFIEL, 2000 REISSUE OF 1900 DESIGN

GERMAN, 1875

Ornate bags have been made from recycled findings for centuries. Victorians sliced up reticules for frame bags, flappers used miser bags to hold gambling chips, and contemporary designers turn to antique frames and trims for the precious gems and workmanship that are rarely available today. This hand-beaded evening bag with a dragon clasp is skirted with a spectacular fringe of round, solid jade beads.

Anthony Luciano, 2001

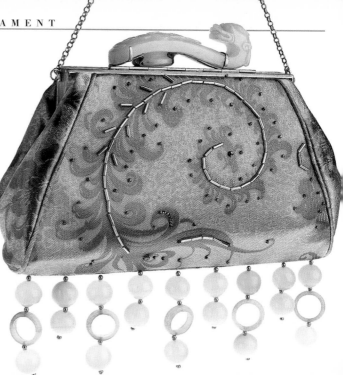

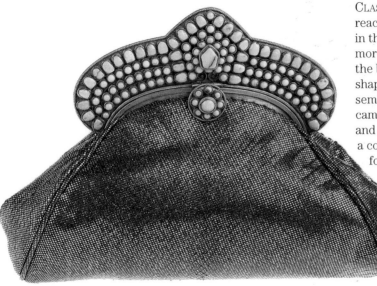

CLASPS AND FRAMES reached a peak of luxury in the 1930s, and the more exotic the materials the better. The crown-shaped clasp of chunky semiprecious stones came from Nepal in 1939 and was remounted onto a contemporary lamé bag for evening.

REVIVALS, 2000

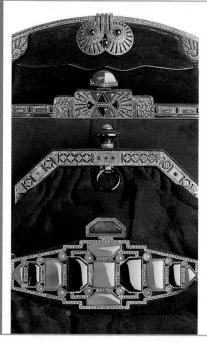

# CLUTCHING AT STYLE: THE ART OF THE CLASP

The features that bring the bag closest to fine jewelry and often fine art are the "hardware" —the frame and clasp. An original clasp sets a bag apart as a precious object. In the 15th century, bags with ornate iron fittings were reserved for the pageantry of religion and hunting. A chunky iron castle clasp mounted on a velvet hunting bag constituted an imposing image of property and power. Ornate gold, silver, and enameled clasps came later, at the end of the 18th century, when the new reticule style adopted neoclassical ornaments, and bags gained more structure. In the 1820s and '30s, when designers and artisans were influenced by all things Greco-Roman, bags featured chains suspended from swan's necks, and classical friezes along their frames.

If the 18th century was the gilded age, the 19th was the age of steel and silver. Cut-steel frames were wed to mourning bags, and intricate, massive cast-silver frames suspended chatelaines from the waist of the Victorian lady. Between 1900 and 1939 the clasp become more and more ornate. Perhaps it was a nostalgic desire for the pomp of royalty that stood threatened by revolution and modernity that made

*French beaded clasps, 1910–25; Far left: Cartier-style clasps, 1930s*

*Valentino Garavani,*
*2001*

*Violette Nozières,*
*2000*

women want tiaras and glittering bags. Clasps were carved in Chinese ivory, and set with semiprecious stones, gigantic rhinestones, and fantastic art nouveau glass by Lalique. In 1923 Egyptomania reached its peak, and the French jewelers Cartier set the standard for art deco decadence with clasps of pavé diamonds, lapis lazuli, and gold scarabs. Mounted on plain black bags, the Cartier style clasp was imitated through the '30s using paste and crystals.

After the deprivation of World War II, there was a hunger for feminine ornament. In October 1948,

British *Vogue* declared it time for "accessories unlimited—no more excuses for making do," and clasps reflected that with wild sculptural shapes in adventurous yet affordable plastics. Now, after a few decades of generic and mass-produced hardware, contemporary designers are returning to unique fittings for bags. Beasts of prey are popular motifs for the dominant luxury labels: Chanel uses a swooping eagle, Fendi a coiling serpent, and Valentino a snake devouring itself. Could these be subliminal symbols of the fierce competition and epic corporate takeovers that dominate the world of high-end handbags?

*Christian Dior Couture, 1997*

OPERATING OUT OF TEXAS, Enid Collins started the craze for cheap little bags screenprinted and studded with stones. Sentimental rather than sophisticated, her bags were cheerful collectibles depicting flowerpots, roadrunners, and friendly owls.

ENID COLLINS, 1960s

> **"No one who was anyone took a handbag to Woodstock."**
> —*Carmel Allen*

THE DAISY was the icon of the pacifist '60s. What's so funny about peace, love, and beaded handbags?

AMERICAN, 1960s

FLOWER POWER. If flowers are the sex organs of nature, then floral handbags must serve the same function in the realm of style. Festooned with ripe blossoms, they make miniature gardens, hinting at fertility and the perpetual promise of spring.

MARIE ART STUDIOS, SHANGHAI, 1930S

ITALIAN, 1910

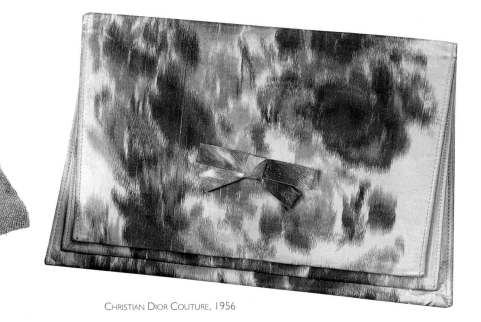

CHRISTIAN DIOR COUTURE, 1956

LIKE A MOTH TO FLAME
or a bee to nectar, the
sensuality of the flower
blossomed lavishly in
art nouveau design.

FRENCH GLASS-BEADED RETICULE, 1910

Trapped between silk and a golden net, this dragonfly has sheer organza wings. Australian designer Belinda Gunn created layers of fragile detail and finished her evening pouch with a strap of amber glass beads strung like a necklace.

Belinda Gunn, 1998

THIS CORD BAG by the American firm Nanette shows the influence of Italian straw, '40s utility wear, and more sophisticated casual day styles.

NANETTE, EARLY 1950s

CRAFT BECAME COOL again in the mid-'90s with knitting and crochet, adding a human touch to corporate style and too many logos.

LORENZA GANDAGLIA, 2001

THE CRAZE FOR CASHMERE
extended to the bag by the
late 19th century. This one
was cut from a shawl,
then hand-beaded.

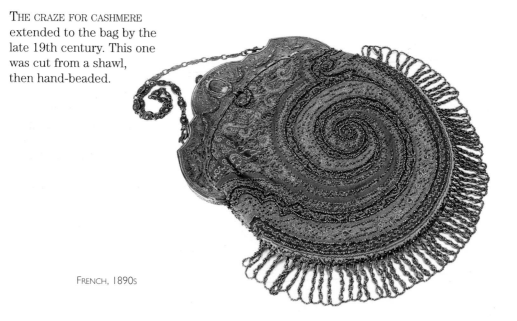

FRENCH, 1890s

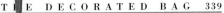

THIS STUPENDOUS FAUX takes a fistful of famous designer looks and mixes them into an unholy cocktail of snakeskin, stainless steel, sari brocade, and fuzzy blue Lurex. What great luxury house would dare claim this bag, spotted in Bangkok, Thailand, as its hybrid offspring?

TANGO, 2000

THE LEATHERWORKERS of Florence and Venice applied traditional crests, gilding, and embossing to handbags made for tourists in the '50s and '60s.

ITALIAN, 1960s

CELTIC- AND OCEANIC-STYLE tattoos were a badge of subcultural initiation in the early '90s. French designer Ursule Beaugeste embosses an undulating Maori pattern onto a pale shoulder bag and creates a somewhat softer ritual ornament.

URSULE BEAUGESTE, 2001

JEAN PAUL GAULTIER put a
19th-century velvet purse
studded with steel beads
at the center of his design
and expanded from there,
adding appliquéd leather,
and a lavish fringe
of beads, leather,
and suede. Even
when worn by
an amazonian
model, this bag
swings well
below the knee.

JEAN PAUL GAULTIER,
1998

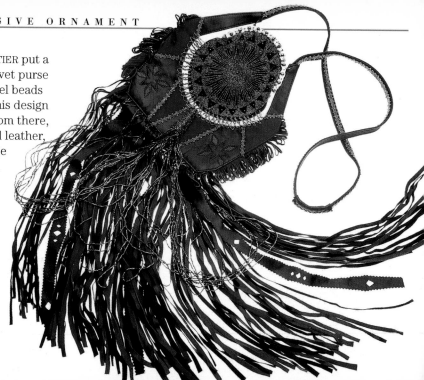

MOROCCAN, 1960

JAMIN AND PUECH
bought a battered
honey-colored shoulder
bag in Morocco and let
it ripen in their atelier.
The fruit? An unlikely
hybrid of decorative
fringe, Mexican cut-work,
and a blue Texas rose.

JAMIN PUECH, 1999

WORN FROM NECK TO NAVEL, an American-Indian beaded bag is vestment, necklace, and utilitarian pouch in one. Studded with tiny glass beads and silk ribbon, it is typical of the fine work that influenced Western embroidery for the rest of the 19th century.

ATTRIBUTED TO CREEK OR SEMINOLE TRIBE, C. 1825

MODERN ART made the leap
to handbags in the '60s with
graphic geometric op-art
designs and pop color.

HANDMADE IN JAPAN FOR
WALBORG, 1969

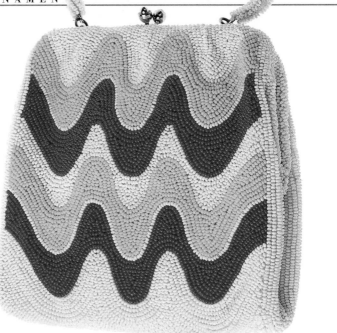

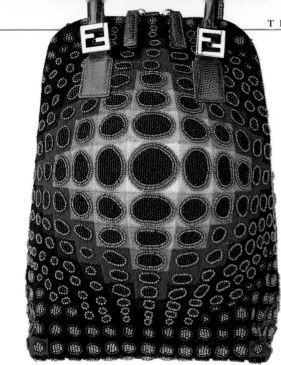

PREGNANT WITH AN IDEA, this elegant evening bag bears the illusion of a rounded belly; the gorgeous optical illusion was influenced by the 1960 paintings of Vasarely.

FENDI, 2000

HOLIDAY STYLE has a way of filtering into high fashion. The exotic beaded designs of Lacroix and Fendi in the '90s owe something to the intensely festooned beach bags of India, the Mediterranean, and beyond.

SPAIN, 1990

# five

# American Classics: Sporty Style

I f Katharine Hepburn were a handbag she might be a brown suede clutch by Koret, luxurious but not fussy. Lauren Hutton, a vast and minimal caramel suede Halston shoulder bag, butter soft with room for adventure. And Jackie? Well, she would have to be a silk satin pochette by Oleg Cassini, sleek, chic, and diplomatically secretive.

The idea that the American woman and her bag are interchangeable is not so absurd. From the sturdy leathers available in the Sears, Roebuck catalogues of the 1890s through to the elegant sportswear spreads featured in *Vogue* in the 1930s, the need to look "pulled together" was always completed by the bag. Gradually growing more and more streamlined, the qualities

*American, 1930;*
*Previous page: Kate Spade, 2002*

we admire in American handbags today—whether a Kate Spade or Lambertson Truex—were established through a process of European influence and local invention. The *sportif* chic of French houses such as Patou and Vionnet were translated by Hollywood into the somewhat masculine pochettes and little clutch bags of Joan Crawford and Norma Shearer. The idea of fashion on the beach, à la Coco Chanel in Deauville, filtered into popular American pattern books with designs for Nantucket baskets and Oriental lantern bags.

The beauty of the American handbag has always

*Lambertson Truex mock zebra, 1999*

*Lambertson Truex, 2001*

been its dance between make-do inventiveness and crazy luxury. Materials like rubber, brass buckles, oilskin, denim, and even telephone cords were borrowed from the hardware store in the forties, an era when ingenuity was respected. The canvas boat bag by L. L. Bean was introduced in 1944 as a gardening tote but quickly became a run-around weekend classic. Casual sporty style was one face of the '50s American handbag, and high glamour was the other. The leopard-skin bag, the accessory that assumed itself more beautiful than the big cat itself, enjoyed popularity by way of Hollywood. Movies like *Mogambo* added to the cachet of a big-game handbag for the urban jungle.

*Lana Marks, 2001*

Whether ferociously chic or simply cheerful and glib, the bag as indispensable accessory survived in American fashion long after hats and gloves faded away. Shades of red, white, and blue have been popular since the 1800s, not only for their obvious patriotic appeal but also for their nautical, military, and polo field associations. Luxury, in a nation of self-starters, has always been linked to leisure.

Yachting canvas and sailing grommets, tennis whites and driving gloves, racing-green suede and linen edged with fine leather are the stuff of aristocrats at play—and such lofty aspirations extend to handbags. Our grandmothers wanted a boxy little Hermès bag with a sensible lock on the front for its whiff of Paris and its no-nonsense East Coast practicality. European chic with a dash of puritan thrift was the embodiment of stealth-wealth style. Deceptively plain designs made of the very finest materials are a particularly American tradition.

*Bonnie Cashin, 1967*

The earliest incarnations of the portable sporty style were products of the war. In the late 1940s, handbag design began to tailor itself to a more mobile, career-minded woman. Thanks to women in the workforce and movie stars striding around in trousers, designers like Claire McCardell and, later, Bonnie Cashin saw

American style as a matter of perpetual movement. Like Charles and Ray Eames, they applied the optimism and clarity of modernism to objects of everyday life. Bags after World War II demanded double if not triple duty. Created for the lady who drove a car, wore bright-red lipstick, and shopped with gusto, bags celebrated a swaggering consumer boom. With smooth lines, luxurious skins, bright color, industrial hardware, and occasionally rustic materials such as gingham and cane, the handbag spoke a brashly vernacular language. After the decade when one bag did for all, the '50s provided giddy diversity; a girl could invest in one important crocodile handbag and still be

*Bonnie Cashin's Double Header, 1970*

*American, 1950s*

tempted by cheap and charming plastic pocketbooks, vinyl patent pochettes, figural cane and velveteen novelty box bags, and petite-point evening bags. Call it the best of times and the worst of times for handbag elegance.

When Bonnie Cashin came along to simplify fashion with her soft leather totes and carry-alls, she provided welcome respite from overly feminine style. She captured the essential sportswear spirit by paring back the bag to its purely functional qualities and by mixing very expensive materials with more informal ones: tweed and denim, kid and canvas. Engaging the bright colors of abstract art and the minimal forms of sculpture, her body bag was little more than a kangaroo pouch, and its shape has echoed through every decade since. In the early '70s Calvin Klein and Halston exploded her vision to vast floppy shoulder bags that fell in elegant folds against jeans

*Judith Leiber lunchbox, 1991*

*Michael Kors, 2002*

and long suede skirts. Michael Kors revived the look again in 2002 with massive egg-shaped totes as big as life buoys.

Sleek geometry and clean, clean lines are key to understanding the American bag, and every designer has his or her own interpretation of the look. For Donna Karan the bag is a vessel for career mobility. Her style lesson of the '80s was first a briefcase and then a backpack for urban success. In the film *Working Girl* Melanie Griffith made the transition to chic urban career girl when she traded in her sloppy suburban shoulder bag for a sleek Donna Karan attaché. Suddenly she was in the elevator going up.

*Donna Karan, 2002*

America's favorite fashion fable is Kate Spade. Born Kate Brosnahan of Kansas City, Missouri, Spade always loved classic style and denies ever having had an experimental "Madonna moment" in high school. Resolute in red lipstick and an Oxford shirt, she went to work as the accessories editor at *Mademoiselle* magazine and invented a tote of her own one weekend in Provincetown, in 1993. Her first bags owed as much to Doris Day as they did to Prada. She took the famous black nylon and made it girlie, creating a boxy little bag, trimmed with daisies and lined with gingham. Her masterstroke was her name, in lowercase type, attached to the front of each bag; it looked like an anti-logo, at once modest and stylishly homegrown. Spade's very simple shapes sprouted into a cult, rousing a new wave of passion for the bag that has not ebbed. It's quite a nice success story and one that forms a tidy portrait of the American spirit in a handbag: If you want something badly enough, you make it yourself, and then, once you succeed, you make it in glazed calfskin in lipstick red.

*Kate Spade,*
*2001*

MOBILITY CREATED THE American handbag. With a sturdy handle and a capacious frame, the first great travelers were carpetbags; designed to move from the stagecoach to the great railroad with both robust practicality and a certain romance.

AMERICAN CARPETBAG, 1850s

ECHOES OF THE CARPETBAG can be seen in the great glossy alligator bags of the '60s, and even Kate Spade's totes.

KATE SPADE, 2002

THE AMERICAN SAMPLER reticule pictured a rigid little house bordered by flowers and a strip of blue sky, and was remarkably unvaried from 1830 to 1890. The only way to date these bags is to study their beads; as the century progressed, beads became larger, patterns coarser, and colors less subtle.

AMERICAN, C. 1870S

THE IDEALIZED VISION OF the frontier is challenged by the American Indian beadwork of the 19th century that depicted a more violent truth.

MINNECONJOU LAKOTA TIPI BAG, 1885

ALTRUISM, HANDICRAFTS, and homespun invention mark the more unusual American bags of the early 1900s. This hand-embossed, soft suede bag bears the crest of Roycroft, an arts and crafts guild that operated in upstate New York from 1895 to 1935.

ROYCROFT, 1900s

1914-1918

FRIENDS of FRANCE

PIOUS AND PICTURESQUE, this cotton pouch is embroidered with the affecting image of a wounded soldier being lifted into a Red Cross ambulance on a road skirted with poplars. It was hand stitched to raise money for relief to France.

AMERICAN, 1920

THE BAG BEGAN AS A POCKET, an object of secret pride and pretty practicality worn beneath petticoats. Eighteenth-century American women made their own with quilting patches and sturdy linen.

AMERICAN, 1780s

POUCHES, POCKETS, and kimono sleeves— all sorts of practical shapes inspired Bonnie Cashin. This simple bag designed to be carried on the forearm was part of Cashin's "grab it and go" sportswear philosophy.

BONNIE CASHIN SLING, 1962

THREE FIRST LADIES all went to Judith
Leiber to get their bags for the inaugural
ball. Laura Bush chose red, Nancy
Reagan white, and Barbara Bush her
signature royal blue.

JUDITH LEIBER, 2001,
1984, 1988

FABERGÉ SINGS "Yankee Doodle Dandy" when Leiber creates a patriotic minaudière.

JUDITH LEIBER, 1998

BADGLEY MISCHKA PAYS homage to the '40s, with a complex crocodile bag in jungle red. The bag is actually a meticulously sculpted pouch; its opening folds forward in a decorative flap held in place by interlocking straps.

BADGLEY MISCHKA, 2002

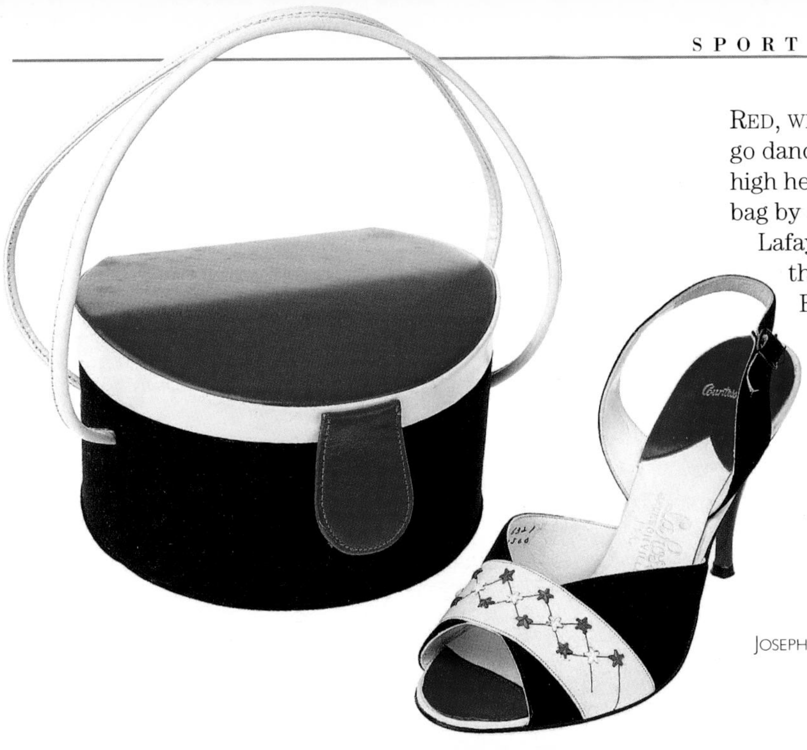

RED, WHITE, AND BLUE go dancing in a sling back high heel and snappy box bag by Joseph La Rose of Lafayette, Florida. Just the ticket for the Fourth of July.

JOSEPH LA ROSE, 1947

MODERNISM STREAMLINED
hardware and gave
the body of the bag
a geometric edge.
This python pochette
bears an exaggerated
buckle clasp, a perfect
example of the influ-
ence of art deco style
on American luxury
bags of the 1930s.

AMERICAN, MID-1930S

KORET WAS THE KINGPIN of popular day bags in the '30s and '40s, producing smart and sometimes surreal designs in durable fabrics like suede and cord. This large bag with a gigantic diaper-pin handle serves as a pun on wartime elegance: safety first.

KORET, 1945

SHOULDERING NEW
RESPONSIBILITIES, leather
bags in wartime adopted
broader straps. New York
designer Anthony Luciano
revives that fashion
moment with a richly
retro mock croc.

ANTHONY LUCIANO,
2001

LANA MARKS claims that her handbag career began when she was invited onto her Majesty Queen Elizabeth's yacht, the *Britannia,* and was confounded in her search for a red alligator bag to match her suit. Marks solved the problem two years later with the hot-pink alligator lunch box that launched her line.

LANA MARKS, 1987

ADVERTISED IN THE SEARS catalogue of 1937 ("They're smart, they're practical, they're easily cleaned!") these bright-striped, wood-beaded bags were cheap and cheerful. They sold for $1.88.

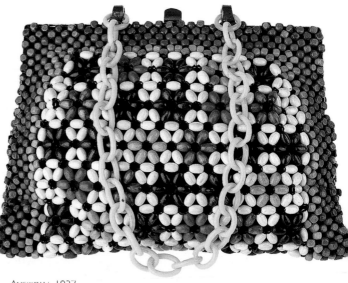

AMERICAN, 1937

AMERICAN DESIGNERS had to invent and make do during World War II, and that spirit of improvisation led them back to a vibrant "peasant" style like that of this ceramic bead and cotton day bag.

AMERICAN, 1940s

FRIEND OR FAUX?
Real zebra was a status
symbol for the '50s
socialite. Walter Kattan
prints a delicious fake,
pairing it with buffed
black calfskin.

WALTER KATTAN, C. 1956

MOCK CROC BECAME an economic necessity for the woman who couldn't afford the real reptile. This clever '60s model snaps open to provide a generous lipstick mirror and a dinghy purse on a chain. Cool on the outside, sensibly suburban within.

AMERICAN, MID-1960s

THE CLASSIC CROCODILE bag by Judith Leiber is deliberately imposing. With a bag this opulent, her dictum that a lady need only carry a lipstick, a comb, and a hundred-dollar bill remains unchallenged.

JUDITH LEIBER, 1991

A TROPHY BAG FOR
A TROPHY WIFE? **Barry
Kieselstein-Cord's** most
famous handbag is both a
blatant display of wealth
(the hardware is eighteen-
karat gold) and a refined
expression of his quirky
sense of humor.

BARRY KIESELSTEIN-CORD, 1990

FROM MANHATTAN WITH LOVE. Anthony Luciano collects vintage clasps, then gives them the shock of the new by pairing them with materials like pink mock python.

ANTHONY LUCIANO, 2002

VIVID COLOR AND BOLD forms were the innovations Bonnie Cashin brought to the career girl's handbag in the '70s—design ideas carried on in the current Coach line.

COACH, 2001
GLOVES BY CASHIN, 1970

# BONNIE CASHIN: POET OF UTILITY

Two American visionaries, Thomas Edison and Bonnie Cashin, shared the same dictum: If it works, it's beautiful. The bags Cashin designed for Coach from 1962 to 1972 live up to that design aesthetic. Brilliantly colored, sturdy, and practical, her shapes make you want to grab them and go—traveling, corporate raiding, or just grocery shopping with élan.

Fascinated by dance and raised playing with silky remnants in her mother's custom dressmaking shop, Cashin developed a passion for sensuous, quality materials transposed onto the moving body. Working as wardrobe mistress for Broadway shows in the '30s, she dressed chorus girls. In the '40s she designed flamboyant costumes for 20th Century Fox, while she herself wore stringently minimal Mao jackets and slim leather. It was a design aesthetic that laid the foundations for American sportswear. Cashin was perpetually

*Classic shopper, 1965*

*Bonnie Cashin in the Coach workshop, 1964. Her chic glamour epitomized the client who carried her bags.*

paring back—putting coin-purse pockets on canvas raincoats, traveling to Asia to collect baskets and textiles, trimming tweed with leather, and yanking the toggles off her convertible sports car to fasten her poncho.

As early as 1954 Cashin was teaming pink and aqua leather and sprigged cotton, denim and silk shantung. When Miles and Lillian Cahn approached her to design accessories for their new company, Coach, in the early '60s, the designer came on board with bags and a manifesto to match. "Make things as lightweight as possible—

*Hero, 1965*

as simple as possible—as punchy as possible—as inexpensive as possible!"

Cashin's first bag for Coach was a portable sling, somewhere between a kangaroo's pouch and a nifty oversized pocket. A coin purse was attached to the outside and it was wittily christened the "Cashin Carry." Next came leather shopping bags in three sizes—large, medium, and dinky.

Based on the paper shoppers she made to haul books and materials to and from her country digs, these bags pulverized the notion that a woman need only carry keys, cash, lipstick, and a hankie. Cashin believed in the dignity of housing "stuff," in wearing three bags on one arm and layering one bag within the other. The contemporary need for satellite bags was anticipated by Cashin's desire to carry bags *à trois*, stacked neatly on

*Totes, 1965*

*"Cashin Carry," 1967*

the forearms and sprouting one or two at the wrist. Bonnie Cashin despised the single black alligator bag. After her visit to India in 1956 she developed her own shade of candy pink and had Coach make up brilliantly hued ice-cream colors in special limited dye runs. Lined with her signature striped madras, Cashin liked proto-pop contrasts and textural wit. "My strong personal feeling," she declared, "is to banish the word 'match'." Acid mustard trimmed in pink, rustic olive-green tweeds edged in lime, and subtle russet reds were her antidotes to stodgy suburban style.

*Cashin drew her ideas directly onto her canvas prototypes, and her sketches were accompanied by copious notes, early 1960s.*

**"I played around with the idea of flatness and packability. All that was really needed was a container to carry all the stuff a girl seems to need."**
—*Bonnie Cashin*

*Double-entry swinger, 1970*

Cashin's shapes were conceived to suit an active woman's life. Deep square shoppers strong enough to be stuffed to the gills with the day's acquisitions, chunky little hobos tough enough to be tossed casually onto the back seat of a car, and the unusually shaped top-zippered hexagon box bag designed with the office in mind. Cashin was obsessed with the relationship between use and form.

For easier access, she slapped pockets on the sides of her Hero lunch box, outfitted the slenderest of evening bags with outlandish front coin pockets, and made her day bag shoulder straps broad and pliable enough not to dig in. By the late '60s her designs were enjoying widespread, low-budget imitation and were delivering a generation of women into the no-fuss liberation of the '70s. For that decade of feminists, a Cashin Coach bag was a low-key

status symbol, both utilitarian and classy.
When Coach revived her 1970 Body bag
for her retrospective at the Fashion
Institute of Technology in New York
in 2000, the bag continued to prove a
revolutionary force—defying froufrou
cocktail purses and fussy fastenings.
Matched with some original '60s
gloves and a vintage Cashin coin
purse, the look is still good to
go. A bag that works like a call
to action.

*Obsessed with utility, devoted to fun,
Cashin spearheaded extra pockets,
saturated color, and satellite bags way
ahead of her time. Safari totes, 1966.*

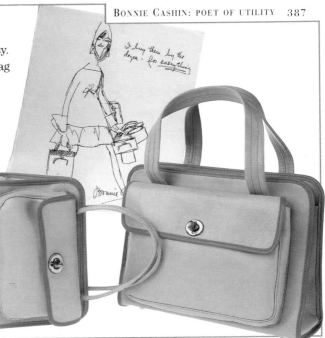

*I buy them by the dozen - for everything*

*Bonnie*

SUMMER PLEASURES TRAVEL in a basket. Inspired by the Italians, who used cane and straw during the post-war leather shortages, Americans fell in love with the woven bag. Worn large à la *Roman Holiday* in the '50s or strewn with plastic pearls, velvet leaves, and plump strawberries in the early '60s, the basket evolved beyond kitsch to a more streamlined form.

AMERICAN, C. 1960

ITALIAN, 1950S

KATE SPADE, 2002

"PRACTICAL ECCENTRICS"
could describe many
American designers.
This anonymous vinyl
and canvas bag from the
1950s was big enough to
hold a pair of galoshes
and came with its own
umbrella. One can only
imagine the matching
raincoat and hat.

AMERICAN, 1950s

L. L. BEAN INVENTED
the rubber-based, leather-
topped "Bean boot," with
a tip like a duck's nose, in
1911. Michael Kors went
one better and slapped a
sturdy rubber sole on his
luxurious day bag. Chunky
and overstated, it was as
practical as a Land Cruiser,
and just as popular.

MICHAEL KORS, 2001

BLUE JEANS WERE the student uniform of '60s campus chic, and bag manufacturers went after the teen market with a zip-front pocket that could be a bookbag or a gym bag.

LEVI STRAUSS, 1960s

THE EVERYDAY BAG SLIPS on like a favorite pair of jeans, well worn, familiar, and artlessly casual.

DOONEY AND BOURKE, 2000

*TRÈS SENSIBLE,* LESPORTSAC was born in Manhattan in 1974. A durable little bag made from ripstop parachute nylon, grosgrain ribbon, and canvas trim, it became a cult bag on the disco scene in the early '80s.

LESPORTSAC, 2001

LeSportsac saw another star turn when Jonathan Adler scrawled his witty "frang-lais" exclamations across the bag in honor of its self-consciously repetitive logo. Feather-light, stackable, and packable, the zippy little pouches provide an affordable alternative to heavy-hitting name-brand bags.

"Le Cute," 2002

THE SUEDE DUFFEL was the "It" bag of the '70s, whose style was tactile, unisex, and sensual. It was heralded by Halston and perfected by Calvin Klein, master of lush, luxe simplicity.

CALVIN KLEIN, 2001

SIMPLICITY is more than just a reduction of elements to their most essential form. In terms of design it is an artful balance between function and our fantasy of what the bag should be.

CALVIN KLEIN, 2002

Funky and folkloric, the '70s combined flower power with hand-painted butch leatherwork for shoulder bags that screamed, "This does not belong to my mother!"

American, early 1970s

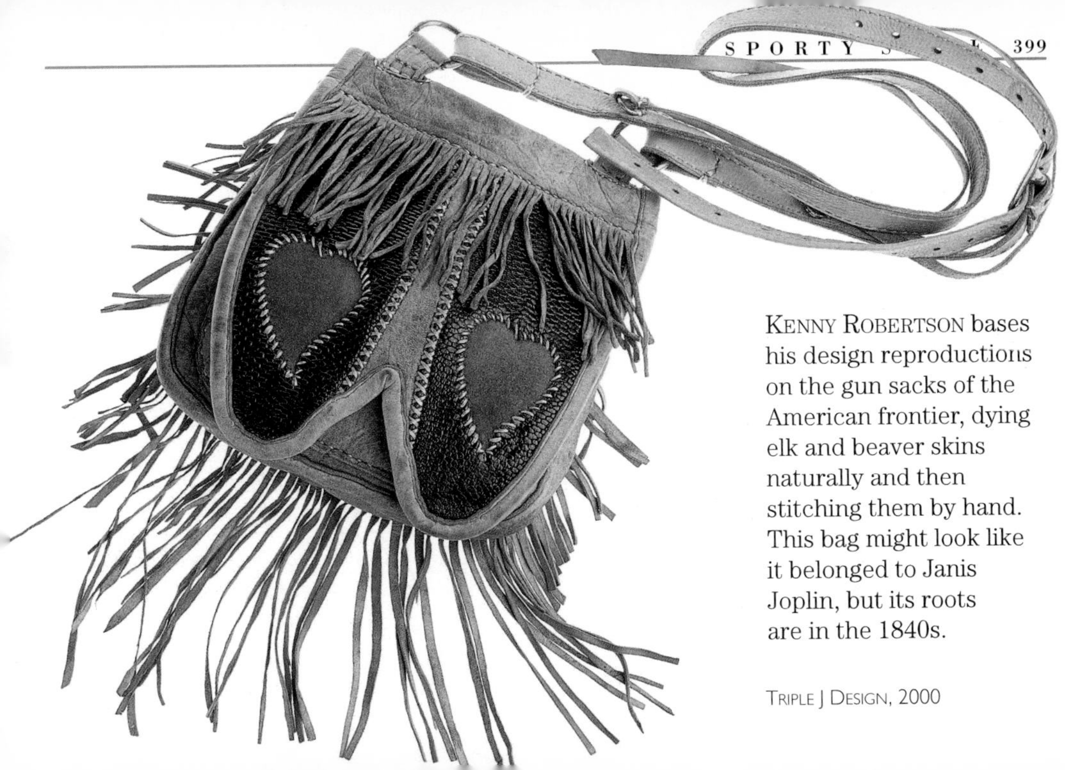

KENNY ROBERTSON bases his design reproductions on the gun sacks of the American frontier, dying elk and beaver skins naturally and then stitching them by hand. This bag might look like it belonged to Janis Joplin, but its roots are in the 1840s.

TRIPLE J DESIGN, 2000

KATE SPADE TAKES A CLASSIC
POCHETTE, not unlike Jackie's
during her Camelot era, and
works it in a burst of
rainbow colors.

KATE SPADE, 2001

"The color, the texture and the sex appeal of the materials are all fundamental to the pleasures of owning a favorite bag, and of having it last."
—*Kari Sigerson &
Miranda Morrison*

MANHATTAN DESIGN DUO Sigerson Morrison are famous for shoes but spent many years obsessing about the perfect bag.

SIGERSON MORRISON, 2002

VISIONS OF FISHING TACKLE, soccer moms, and school ties are roused by the heavily buckled, saddle-stitched, riveted, and trimmed bags of Dooney and Bourke, designed and made in Connecticut, home of all of the above.

DOONEY AND BOURKE, 2001

INSTANT CLASSICS that look hauntingly familiar— that's the trick to creating something new with a vintage resonance. Marc Jacobs owes his massive buckles and chunky space-age styling to Courrèges and '60s tailoring, but he has made the look his own. The beauty of American design is not just that property is theft, but that practice makes perfect.

MARC JACOBS, 2002

# THE BAG THAT WENT TO WORK

**S**tuffed to capacity and hauled back and forth in an endless cycle of duty and diligence, nothing burdens or liberates a woman more than the bag she takes to work. Quintessential New York designer Donna Karan tells a tale about her work bag being so heavy that she had her driver deliver it while she jogged to the office on foot. The notion of a bulging briefcase belonging to a female executive strikes a bold contrast to the dainty leather handbags of Victorian ladies.

With the right to work came the right to carry a working bag, and as female professional responsibility expanded, so did the size of the sack.

We can thank the early feminists for the leather shoulder bag. Adapted from postal satchels and hunting bags, the stout, square leather envelope was worn diagonally across the body by suffragettes, who needed their hands for pamphleteering. In the '20s and '30s office girls carried pochettes, square envelope bags

*American postal bag, early 1900s*

similar to the leather document wallets women wore in the 18th century. But with World War II came a greater range of work and a more pragmatic approach to the bag. Wartime women rode bicycles, took on men's jobs, and needed their hands free to do it. Broad, sensible shoulder bags, made of plastic or of standard military-issue canvas, were the precursors to the classic work bags most women carry today.

Handbag design pioneer Bonnie Cashin insisted on a capacious hobo or fabric shopper with shoulder straps, and began making her own as early as 1955, but the shoulder bag didn't become almost an office uniform until the early '70s.

*American secretarial pocketbook, 1930s*

*Bonnie Cashin, 1978*

Whether it was an L. L. Bean canvas tote crammed with papers, a LeSportsac nylon pouch, or a classy Coach in richly colored leather, a bag on the shoulder was a sign that women were bonded (physically as well as socially) to their work. In stark opposition to the conventional handbag, the utility bag of the '70s symbolized everything practical and action-packed. In true feminist spirit, the bag was now a tool rather than a mere decoration.

By the slick and corporate '80s, the Annie Hall look—a battered, slouchy hobo stuffed to the gills—looked dated. We didn't want just bags anymore, we wanted systems. Donna Karan was one of the first to promote the idea of the satellite bag, with a briefcase for day housing a smaller bag for lunch trips and evening. Practicality became wedded to style in the '80s when fitness, jogging, and corporate climbing made the backpack (and sneakers) almost a career woman's uniform. Launched in 1985, the Prada backpack of black ripstop nylon was a joyous alternative to the engorged attaché and could contain the modern micro-office of filofax, pager, and pen. Donna Karan, Chanel, and Hermès made popular, upscale versions.

*Guy Laroche, 1969*                *La Baggagerie, 1970s*                *Dooney and Bourke, 1978*

The '90s working girl flirted with androgynous and futuristic styles: the messenger bag, the fanny pack, the belt pouch, and versions of Bonnie Cashin's pouchlike "Body" bag for Coach, but the style that still reigns supreme is the mother ship and dinghy. Bags within bags have become the norm for women who need a life beyond work. Lambertson Truex's buffed leather bag is big enough for a laptop and an evening bag. Ferragamo put a zippered compartment in the base of their handbags in 2001 for an extra set of shoes and a skinny clutch. The weekend bag has become popular for the office because it affords the notion of escape, even on a Monday. If we love the idea of the satellite bag breaking free of the huge meta-office with straps, it is mainly because it is tiny and graceful—qualities that a work bag can never truly possess.

*Prada, 1986*

*Ferragamo, 2001*

*Lambertson Truex Westport tote and evening bag, 2001*

THE TOTE HAS BECOME a part of our national costume. Beginning with the first L. L. Bean canvas boat bag in 1944, we have come to rely on the tote for travel, for work, and for concealing the mess of everyday life.

L. L. BEAN, 2002

PATCH, "DOWNTOWN GIRL'S TOTE," 2001

KATE SPADE, "UPTOWN GIRL'S TOTE," 2002

WEST MEETS EAST in
American luxury bags
based on Asian classic
designs.

NATORI, 2002

# six

# Novelty & Caprice: Handbag Humor

**D**esigned to amuse, a novelty bag is like red shoes on a rainy day—impractical and absolutely fabulous. Shaped like a jelly bean, a book, an accordion, or a loaf of bread, the novelty bag pushes the artistic language of the handbag into the realm of theater. Unusual material, clever shapes, and bizarre clasps and handles celebrate the idea that a bag can be a whimsical ruse, a conversation piece or, like a great shoe, a cheeky sex object.

Decadent and decorative, novelty bags sprout up in expansive times—when the marketplace is more diverse and playful, and when a wealth of new materials invites design experimentation. Elizabethan novelty bags shaped like animals, grapes, and nuts created drama for their wearers. Like props in a play, they accompanied the exotic feather headdresses

*Elizabethian frog bag, 16th century; Previous page: American, 1915–20*

*Priscilla Snyder, 1994*

and fans to the masque. Carrying a scented "sweet purse" (a small pouch to perfume your skirts) in the shape of a leaping frog also conveyed a certain learned sophistication, mimicking the natural world with a flourish of fashion.

With symbolism comes spice. In the 17th century, newlyweds exchanged wedding bags, each cast with a porcelain portrait, one of the bride and one of the groom. As miniature symbolic dowries from both the man and the woman, these one-of-a-kind bags became an extension of their owners, a strange mix of material possession and sentimental attachment. A bag bearing a woman's face stuffed with coins was a powerful symbol of exchange and ownership, effectively saying, "With this bag I thee wed." Soft, round, and replete with bounty, wedding bags were modern good-luck charms with ancient meanings, the

*Limoges,*
*c. 1690s*

*German, 1860*

purse long represented receptive female genitals, and replaced the male codpiece (where once a man's money was stored) as a symbol of masculine power and material prestige.

In the late 18th and early 19th centuries the favorite novelty bag was the souvenir purse. A silk reticule with hand-painted lithographs of the Parisian monuments or a box bag hand-enameled with Viennese streetscapes was a portable photo album that showed off a recent trip to the Continent. The Victorians did not go for figural or novelty bags; their day bags were pragmatic, and their evening bags overstuffed and sentimental. It took shorter skirts and wilder times for the bag to be able to laugh at itself. Flappers were happy to carry their party trappings in a porcelain doll bag whose ruffled skirts concealed a silky interior or to use a little fur dog as a cigarette case.

*Katherine Baumann, Titanic bag, 1999*

The golden age of the novelty bag came in the 1930s. The decade that produced screwball comedy, Bakelite, tap dancing, and surrealism inspired quirky bags. Created for an intellectual elite, Elsa Schiaparelli's bird-cage bag and folded newspaper bag brought on a powerful trend for figural bags. Suddenly everyone wanted a bag modeled after the shape of something utterly modern and zany. A leather clutch shaped like the *Queen Mary*, the Daimler automobile, the Lindbergh plane. Like a favorite soft toy, a figural pochette could be held close to the body, striking a witty contrast to a sober little suit.

*Moschino, 2001*

Wartime did not cool the passion for bizarre bags, especially as surrealist dreams filtered into magazine illustrations and department store windows. The profusion of clock motifs on bags was probably triggered by Dali's melting watch, and Anne Marie's opera bag shaped like a mandolin suggests Magritte's famous pipe. Witty and provocative, novelty bags provided welcome respite from sensible shoulder straps and rations. They were also the perfect collectible for American tourists and GIs visiting Paris after the war. By the mid-'50s, poodle-shaped bags in glossy black cane, lurid love hearts in hot-pink velvet, and "message" bags listing loves, hates, and snatches of rock-and-roll, heralded a riotous age of kitsch and were the result of designers marketing to a new teenage market. If the '30s look was a modernist socialite, the '50s look was her delinquent daughter; its bags owed more to Walt Disney than Marcel Duchamp.

Overtly feminine and frivolous, a bag in the shape of a flowerpot, a corset, or a cake appeals to the sort of woman who shops for eccentric pleasure. The economic boom of the '80s, coupled with the era's postfeminist passion for everything '50s, brought the novelty bag back with a vengeance. Jean Paul Gaultier, fueled by horror films and London punk style, took a long black glove or a miniature coffin to make his spooky evening clutches. Franco Moschino rebelled

*American, 1950s*

against the starchy signora style of the Italian handbag by using Popeye and Olive Oyl, pastries and pasta as ingredients for his novel confections. His most famous bag transforms polished brown calfskin into a gâteau covered in melting chocolate. British designer Lulu Guinness took a leaf from Schiaparelli's book and created an iconic little black flowerpot bag sprouting vermilion roses.

*Lulu Guinness, 2001*

Putting irony before formality, novelty handbags provide a cleansing force when fashion gets too stuffy, too minimal, or just plain stagnant. Imagine Diana Vreeland posing for *Harper's Bazaar* in 1942 with a leopard-print bag shaped like a Russian muff or Bjork tripping down the red carpet at Cannes cradling a Judith Leiber polar bear and you can appreciate the refreshing role of absurd style. Sometimes looking faintly ridiculous is the most sophisticated gesture of all.

ELIZABETH ARDEN sends
a message with a twisted
love heart in ruched
velvet. Sweet, funny
Valentine, you make
me smile with my heart.

ELIZABETH ARDEN,
EARLY 1950S

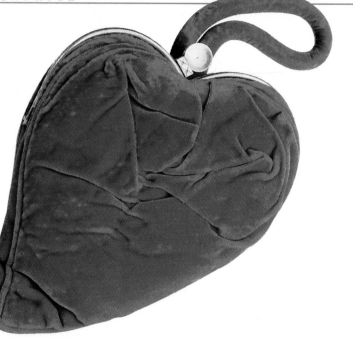

POSSIBLY THE MOST ICONIC (and famous) of all Moschino's novelty bags, this polished calfskin gâteau declares, "Fudge the fashionistas, let them eat cake."

MOSCHINO, 1996

TOWERING LIKE A MARZIPAN *BONBONNIÈRE*, this hand-made silk bridal bag is not about to get tossed to the bridesmaids. Connecticut designer Joy Liotta considers them "bridal heirlooms to be passed down through the generations."

GIOIA, 2000

AFTER THE WEDDING, THE HONEYMOON, and to celebrate, a bottle of Reims champagne in a black suede bucket complete with plastic ice cubes.

ANNE MARIE OF FRANCE, MID-1940s

JEAN PAUL GAULTIER explodes the notion of the quiet little clutch with his Bracelet de Force. In patent leather, the bag moves into the realm of bondage.

JEAN PAUL GAULTIER, 2001

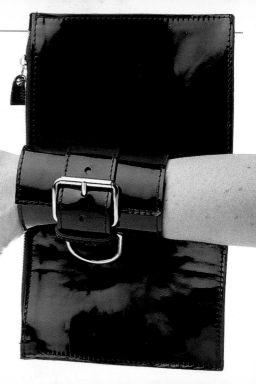

"I want to create theater, clothes are theater."
—*Jean Paul Gaultier*

JEAN PAUL GAULTIER
GLOVE BAG, 1998

ANNE MARIE OF FRANCE made witty figural bags with remarkable interiors and openings. The "drum" bag opened into two completely separate compartments, and the rolltop bag opened with a concertina lid just like a rolltop desk. With mock clock faces and telephone receivers, these were the first of the fabulous faux.

ANNE MARIE OF FRANCE, STAND-UP PIANO, RADIO, CLOCK, POWDER PUFF, DRUM, ROLLTOP DESK, KIOSK, AND TELEPHONE BAGS, 1945–LATE 1950s

SOME OF THE MOST BEAUTIFUL BAGS in the world carry nothing more than an idea. This solid wood attaché case hewn from lumber scraps evokes a deconstructed building or a portable city grid.

BARBARA ANDREWS, 1999

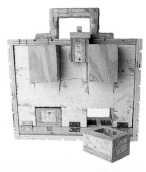

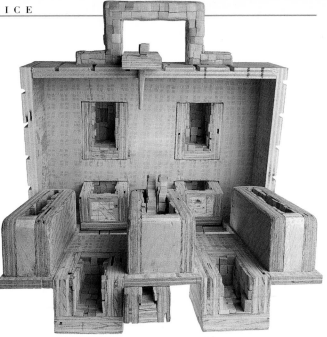

HANSEL AND GRETEL don't live here anymore. Decked out with a red lamé roof, a pink python front door, and yellow suede walls, this Moschino gingerbread house lives up to his quip "If you can't be elegant, at least be extravagant."

MOSCHINO, 2000

MOSCHINO WAS A PACIFIST and pop anarchist; his smiley-face bag updates the icon of the '70s, begging fashion editors to lighten up.

MOSCHINO, 1994

FASHION MAGAZINES in the '50s loved to feature lists of dos, don'ts, and why nots. This bag offers glamour-girl logic du jour.

FABRIQUÉ, 1950s

Teenagers in the 1950s had spending power for the first time in history. Who else would blow their pocket money on a basket bedecked with athletic mice and Astroturf?

Wickley, late 1950s

THE TRAVEL SOUVENIR, the toy, and the sentimental collectible merged in the handbag look of the '50s. Women were not ashamed to walk down the street with a gaudy bag that looked like a carnival prize.

FLORIDA HANDBAGS, 1950s

SALVATORE FERRAGAMO'S most erotic shoe might just be his prow-toed ankle boots. Taking a trio of these shoes from 1930 to 1935, the house created a bag that mimics a charm bracelet.

FERRAGAMO, 1991

NOVELTY COMES IN THREES. Three little velvet purses suspended from a clear plastic bracelet is the '50s interpretation of a medieval chatelaine, the bag that used to hang from the hip of the lady of the house.

RYNOR TRIO BRACELET BAG, LATE 1940S

BEFORE POP ART CAME
SURREALISM, the art
movement spearheaded
by intellectuals and
beloved by bag designers.

WALKFORT, ALLIGATOR
SAFETY-PIN BAG,
EARLY 1950S

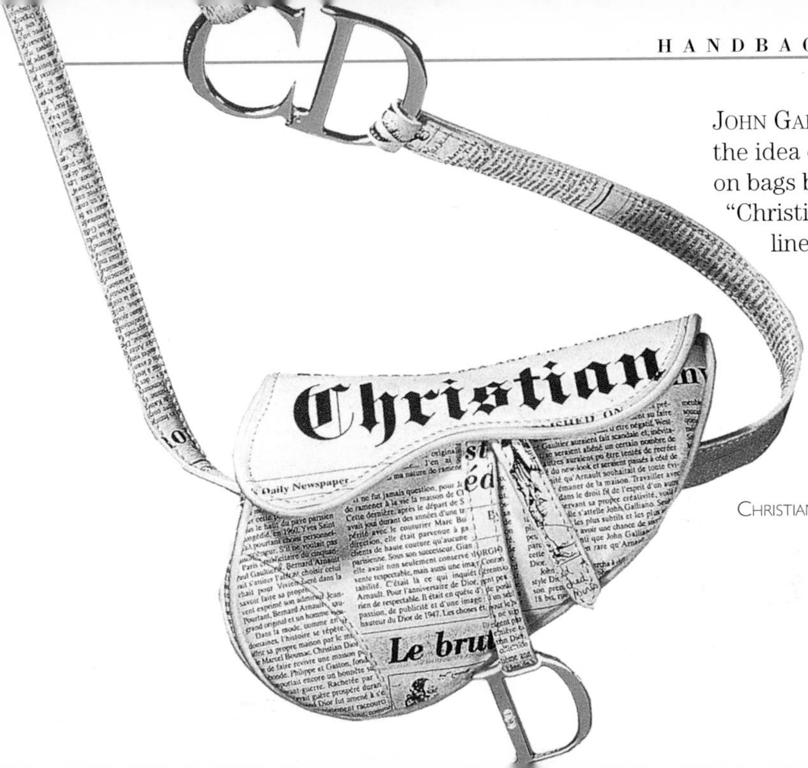

JOHN GALLIANO UPDATES the idea of using newsprint on bags by emblazoning "Christian Dior" in headline letters.

CHRISTIAN DIOR, 2000

FEMININE IMAGERY IN THE '80S was given a postfeminist twist when corsets, flowers, and lace became badges of power. Is it surprising that Madonna was one of the first collectors of this rich velvet flowerpot bag?

LULU GUINNESS, 1997

"COME UP AND SEE ME SOMETIME," cooed the sexy little powder-puff bags with lingerie straps in the late '80s.

JAMIN PUECH, 1989

THE BAG AS PERSONALIZED MEMENTO. Anya Hindmarch created a limited edition of celebrity snapshot totes to raise money for charity. Manolo Blahnik chose Monty, the little Scottie dog who was his muse for twenty years, to adorn his bag.

ANYA HINDMARCH, 2002

DONNA MAY BOLINGER,
2002

STYLISH IN A PINCH, erotic art becomes the handbag, in a collage based on the Renaissance portrait *Gabrielle D'Estrées and Her Sister in the Bath.*

TRAVELING SALESMEN in the 19th century didn't just use catalogues to peddle their wares. This minute leather sample (shown actual size) is realistic down to the tiny silver rivets and sturdy frame.

GERMAN, 19TH CENTURY

AS SMALL AS A CHILD'S PALM, miniature coin purses with painted porcelain faces were treasured curios in the early 19th century.

GERMAN, C. 1830

# ELSA SCHIAPARELLI: THE MAD HATTER

"It's only tinsel, trash, hardware, street fair, showing off!" Elsa Schiaparelli said of her own designs, but what exquisite tinsel and what ingenious trash. Born in Rome to nobility in 1890, Schiaparelli turned fashion inside out, making hats out of shoes and bags out of birdcages. A bundle of stylish contradictions, Schiaparelli didn't sew and barely sketched, but had an uncanny ability to get others to translate her visions into cult objects. Her entrée into French fashion in 1927 was a trompe l'oeil sweater that featured a big white bow on the décolletage drawn cartoon-flat like Fritz the Cat. Created by a troupe of Armenian knitters, her first collection made an instant splash, combining home-spun execution with sophisticated concepts— absurdist fashion, gift-wrapped. Her handbags retained a strong sense of practicality no matter how fantastic their concepts became; for day her double-decker work bag opened into two distinct compartments, one on top of the other. And for night

*Pansy evening bag, 1937*

she created a gold and silver lamé evening purse designed to hang around the neck like a tram conductor's bag. Her cotton newsprint bag (bearing press clips of herself!) was the first-ever customized designer fabric, and from a distance it looked exactly like a folded copy of *Le Monde*.

Like her contemporary Diana Vreeland, Schiaparelli was a baroque modernist, snobbish about the splendor of the past but savagely committed to new materials and modernity. The audacity of her vision was inspired by the surrealists who became her friends. Salvador Dali helped her create an electric evening bag in 1938, featuring Dali's line drawings embossed into the gold-plated interior of the bag; the backlit lipstick mirror was illuminated by tiny

*Newsprint bag, 1934*

lightbulbs that switched on whenever the bag was opened. Rich women snapped up her work, eager to "wear" the ideas of the day. Some might say that Schiaparelli's handbags were the most accessible ready-mades that contemporary art ever produced, avant-garde objects with a function.

*The Lanterne bag, detail*

*The Lanterne bag, with Salvador Dali, 1938*

"It was the time when Dadaism and Futurism were the talk of the world," said Schiap, "when it was not done to ask what a painting represented or what a poem meant." In that maverick spirit she employed the best artists to realize her ideas. Jean Cocteau drew sleeping nymphs for her evening capes, the artist Jean Clement made her bags in candy-colored plastics, the designer Roger Model carved out her most sculptural leather bags, and master embroiderer Albert Lesage translated her allegorical visions in beetle wings, spun-glass flowers, and embossed gold thread. As the surrealist object was an exercise in displacement, the handbag became the perfect vehicle for erotic puns. Schiaparelli made a music box bag that trilled when opened and a transparent plastic evening bag in the shape of a beautifully curved abalone shell.

At the height of her artistic collaborations in the late '30s, Schiaparelli presented four incredible collections. The Circus show was replete with performing horses, acrobats, elephants, and balloon handbags shaped like inverted question marks. The Pagan collection was based on Botticelli, with mythological creatures trailing bouquet bags of pansies and violets. The third show cast visual imagination into the heavens with the signs of the Zodiac. The last collection, shown just before the French occupation, was inspired by the commedia dell'arte, and featured satin patchwork, ribbons, bright Italianate color, and

*Seashell bag made by Coppola and Toppo for Schiaparelli, early 1950s*

harlequin bags in shades of pink and blue. Some may question Schiaparelli's decision to send in the clowns when the world was on the brink of war, but humor was her primary artillery against dictators and bad design.

Throughout the war Schiaparelli boosted morale by designing witty rayon blouse and bag sets printed with ration tickets, a portable

> **"In difficult times, fashion is always outrageous."**
> *—Elsa Schiaparelli*

trousseau in a handbag, and bags to lightly skirt the waist and the wrist. An international traveler, she saw the bag as a mutable, intimate

accomplice. No matter what the social climate, she believed that a woman should never be stripped of the dignity of carrying her own handbag even if it was just an improvised basket thrown together with canvas and straw like the ones she carried during the occupation.

International licensing, designing for Hollywood, and working closely with large American department stores took Schiaparelli away from her experimental design of the 1950s. Her style became more subdued and she became better known for perfumes than for the sensible day bags that

*Harlequin, 1939*

still carried her name. In 1954 she closed shop in Paris. In her memoir, *Shocking Life,* she wrote about the transformation of the couture bag from artistic curiosity to market force. "Artists," she wrote ruefully, "took much more part in the life and development of fashion than they do today. . . . At that time it was not a matter of pure advertising interests: of who bought and how widely a model could be reproduced. The present system tends to produce dullness."

Elsa Schiaparelli's ideas were radical because they looked so different and worked so well. Her bizarre couplings of modern and ancient materials, displaced sculptural elements, and her taste for bags with waistlines, ribbons, and roses set the trend for all figural bags to come. Although revived, borrowed, and blatantly stolen by the '80s designers who fell in love with surrealist fashion, her originality was never quite replicated by anyone else. Why just be beautiful, her designs seemed to ask, when you can be shocking?

*Silk satin embroidered by Lesage, late 1930s*

POETIC BUT EVER PRAGMATIC, Schiaparelli fused fantastic form and functional ease. Her ingenious "double" handbag predicted the compartmental bag well before the war, and her elegant basket bag in ruched leather concealed a cavernous interior within its wasp-waisted curves.

BOTH BAGS ROGER MODEL FOR ELSA SCHIAPARELLI, MID-1930s

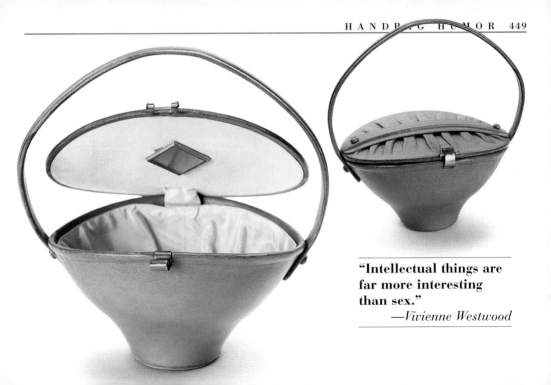

"Intellectual things are
far more interesting
than sex."
—*Vivienne Westwood*

LULU GUINNESS gives us the mansion without the mortgage, perfect for a girl whose home is her handbag.

LULU GUINNESS,
2000

THE ART DECO DELANO Hotel rises like an ocean liner on the horizon of Miami's South Beach. This bag remains a best-seller in the hotel's ritzy gift shop.

LULU GUINNESS, 2000

PASTA, THE CULTURAL
CURRENCY OF ITALY,
is used by Moschino to
ridicule export mentality,
high fashion, and mass
production. Stop the fashion
system! Wake up and smell
the spaghetti!

MOSCHINO, 1999

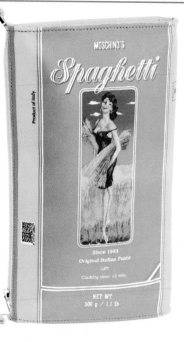

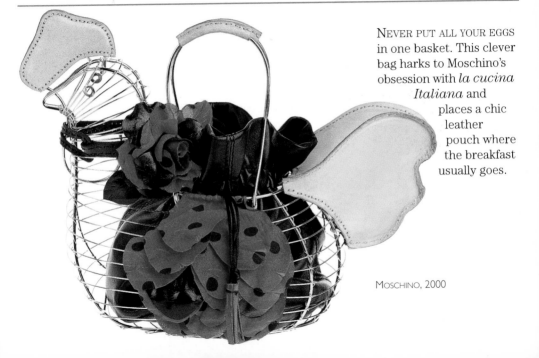

NEVER PUT ALL YOUR EGGS in one basket. This clever bag harks to Moschino's obsession with *la cucina Italiana* and places a chic leather pouch where the breakfast usually goes.

MOSCHINO, 2000

WAY BEFORE MODERNISM, a handbag could be as witty as the woman who carried it. This 200-year-old reticule illustrates the wild streak in post-revolutionary French design.

FRENCH, 1800-10

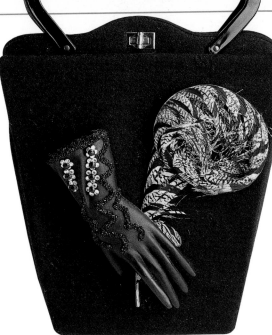

ANATOMY BECAME FRAGMENTED in the hands of the surrealists, and everything from a glove to a feather took on a symbolic charge. This suede handy bag speaks less of the power of the unconscious and more about shopping power.

AMERICAN, 1940s

LIMITED-EDITION ART BAGS of the late '60s captured the *esprit de jour* of student politics, intellectual whimsy, and subtle sex appeal. The text of this bag reads more like a line from a Godard film than from a page of *Paris Vogue*.

SOME DAY YOU MAY CHANCE TO LOOK IN THIS PRIVATE LITTLE BOOK IN IT YOU ARE APT TO FIND SNATCHES OF MY SECRET MIND- SWATCHES OF LOVE AND LIFE AND SUCH- THOUGHTS THAT DON'T MEAN VERY MUCH TO ANYONE - EXCEPTING ME BEST CLOSE IT UP AND LET IT BE!

STRICTLY PERSONAL

FRENCH SATIN BOOK BAG, 1969

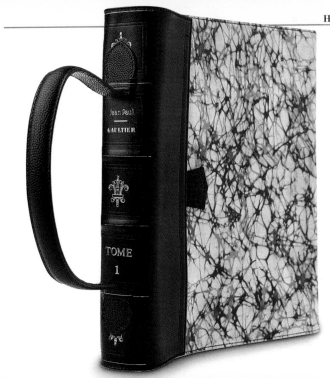

A BAG OF BIBLICAL proportions rewrites the book on drama queen accessories.

JEAN PAUL GAULTIER, 1993

THE FLOWER POT BAG was born with the surrealists and has been blooming ever since. Add silk roses and carry in the sun.

MALI PARMI, 2001

THE FRENCH POODLE ruled fashion from the '30s to the early '60s, selling Parisian style to the world.

VALBORO, C.
1938

EVEN IF YOU'VE NEVER seen the Left Bank
or the Mojave Desert, you can still own
the souvenir. In the 1950s,
exotic-destination
bags traveled from
Paris, France, to
Paris, Texas.

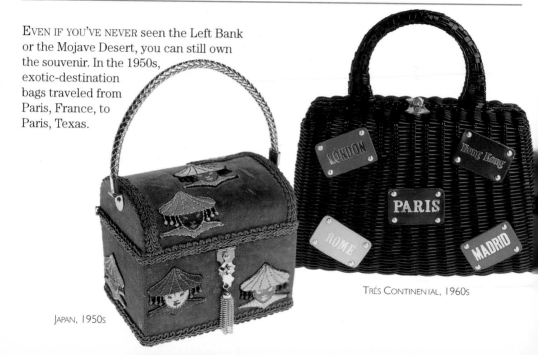

TRÉS CONTINENTAL, 1960S

JAPAN, 1950S

AMERICAN, 1950S

AMERICAN, 1950S

MAGI, ARIZONA LUNCH BOX, 1950S

ELSA SCHIAPARELLI'S most
famous early surrealist
bag was made from
a birdcage, no doubt
inspired by the collages
of Max Ernst. This black
felt aviary by Anne Marie
of France takes a more
stylized approach.

ANNE MARIE OF FRANCE,
1940s

SECRETIVE AND REVEALING, a closed book and a fastened handbag share the appeal of privacy and transgression. A woman carries her bag close, like a journal, filling it with a mixture of the banal, the intimate, and the startlingly personal.

PALOMA PICASSO BOOK BAG, 1980s

MASCULINE TOYS, FEMININE PLEASURES: Three very different takes on the football pass the handbag from Mali, Africa (where it was fashioned from papier-mâché), to the couture salons of Moschino and Chanel.

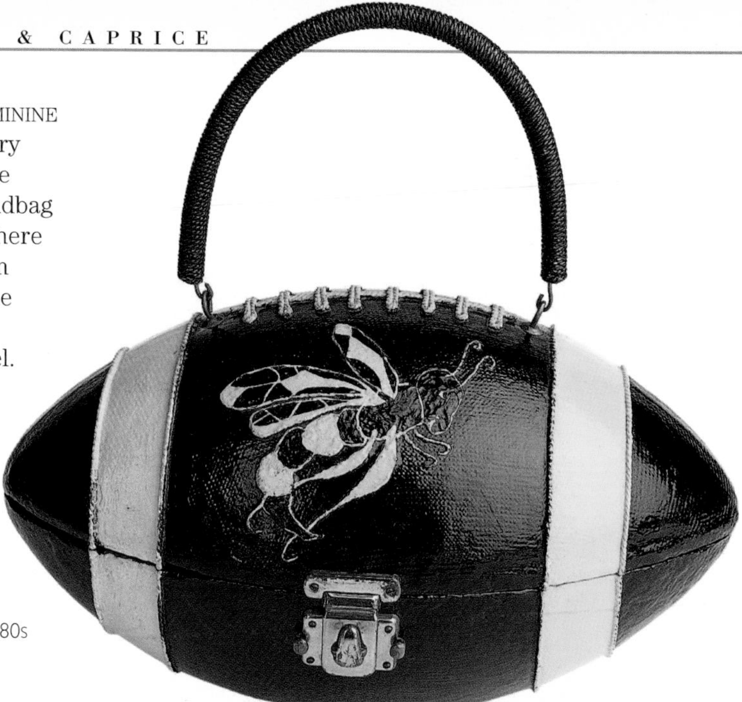

MADE IN MALI, 1980s

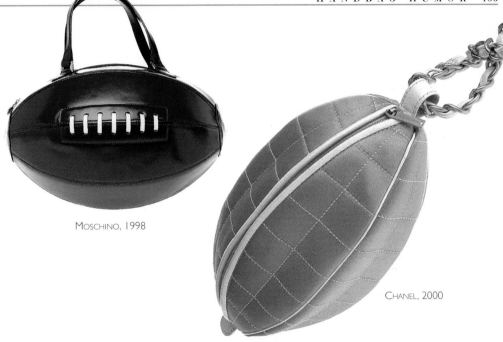

MOSCHINO, 1998

CHANEL, 2000

THE CORSET PREOCCUPIED European fashion in the mid-1980s. Karl Lagerfeld made one into a hat, Jean Paul Gaultier fashioned one into a dress, and Moschino stole his inspiration from Sophia Loren and created a backpack.

MOSCHINO BUSTIER BACKPACK, 1985

TAILORS' DUMMIES and headless torsos were the stuff of Giorgio De Chirico's and Salvador Dali's paintings in the '30s. In the '40s they appeared in countless fashion illustrations and window displays, and by the '50s the theme was carried onto handbags.

ITALIAN, C. 1950

FAST FOOD BECOMES glamour to go—trashy, flashy, and pure fun.

KATHERINE BAUMANN, 1990s

MOSCHINO, 2001

KATHERINE BAUMANN,
1990s

AMERICAN,
1980s

HANDBAG AND HOUSEHOLD names collide in a bag shaped like history's most famous plane. Created in Germany just one year after Charles A. Lindbergh's maiden voyage across the Atlantic.

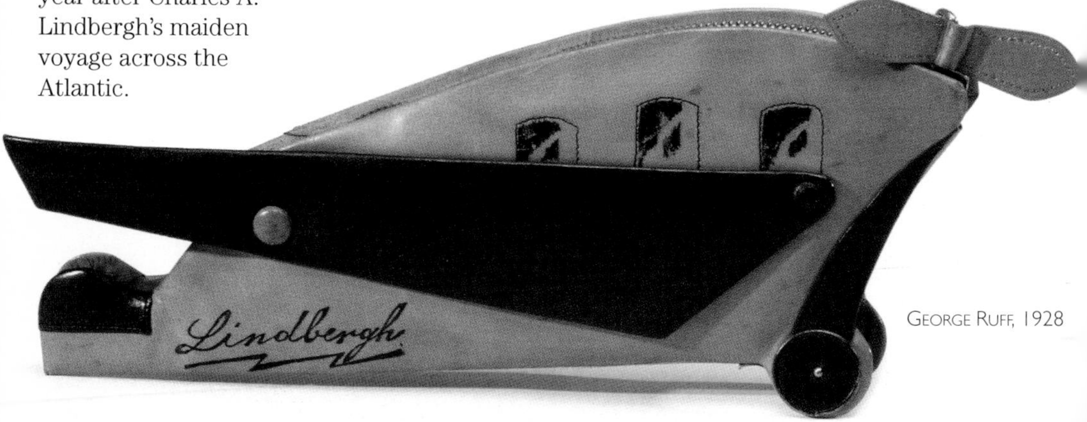

GEORGE RUFF, 1928

SOLD ABOARD THE
SS *Normandie* in 1935,
this modest little bag has
a steam funnel for a
clasp. Bags in the shape
of cars and airplanes
dominated the 1930s,
the optimistic machine
age of sports cars,
skyscrapers, and
soaring industry.

FRENCH, 1935

OLIVE OYL AND POPEYE
were Moschino's favorite
couple. Perhaps this
cherry red boxing glove
belonged to Brutus.

MOSCHINO, 2001

JEAN CHARLES DE CASTELBAJAC likes to engage the body in all of his designs. His oversized baseball mitt shoulder bag wraps around the waist, turning fashion into a spectator sport.

JEAN CHARLES DE CASTELBAJAC, 1984

BEFORE THE CELL, there was the telephone bag, a cult object from the 1960s that actually plugged into a wall jack and operated as a working phone.

DALLAS HANDBAGS, 1970S

THIS '80S RADIO BAG is wired for sound with Walkman headphones and room for disco roller skates. Not all fad bags were bestsellers: note the radical markdowns scrawled onto the original price tag.

AMERICAN RADIO BAG, EARLY 1980S

THE VICTORIANS HAD A TASTE for bestiaries, enclosing stuffed owls in glass domes and their spare change in a nasty set of alligator claws. Fox stoles had glass eyes in the '20s, and even muffs had frightening little faces festooned on their fronts. The crocodile bag was a huge fad in the '30s and it came with Bakelite handles and little claw paws.

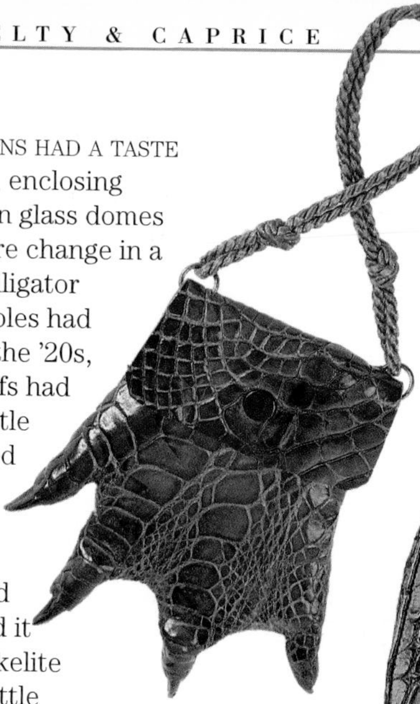

AMERICAN CROCODILE PURSE, 1930s

ENGLISH AI LIGATOR PURSE, 1890s

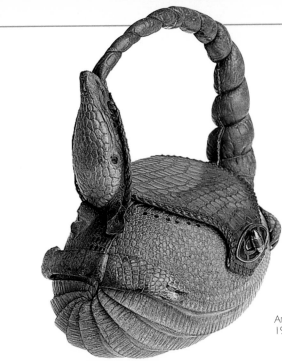

"Fashion is a form of ugliness so intolerable it must be changed every six months."

—*Oscar Wilde*

AMERICAN ARMADILLO BAG, 1950s

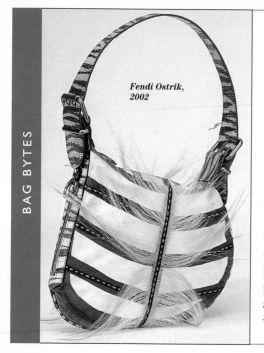

*Fendi Ostrik, 2002*

# THE "IT" BAG

Track any decade in the 20th century and you will find an "It" bag, the single accessory that defined the era. Some bags are born with "It" and some have "It" thrust upon them, being named after the celebrities who carried them. In the '50s, of course, it was Grace Kelly's bag that launched the whole "It" trend. In the '60s it was Paco Rabanne's metallic paillette shoulder bag, designed to literally swing. The '70s saw the return of the monogrammed status handbag, with Gucci and Fendi sporting caramel and chocolate logos and brassy insignia. In the '80s the flashy Chanel bag and the sensible Prada backpack shared the crown of "It." But come the '90s and the battle for "It" intensified to the point where a new bag was hailed each season as the

*Balenciaga Saddlebag, 2002*

One. Some say that the proliferation of experimental design always comes at the end of one century and the beginning of another. This was true

*Sonia Rykiel Domino, 2001*

of handbags in the 1790s, when they morphed from pockets and blousy work bags to reticules, and in the 1890s, when the leather handbag, the beaded bag, the silver mesh bag and the chatelaine were coveted simultaneously and all were considered the epitome of "It."

Just before the turn of this century the frenzy for "It" bags reached critical mass. In 1996 it was the Kate Spade tote; in 1998 we obsessed over the Fendi baguette and the Chanel 2005. In '99 it was the Prada bowling bag and the Vuitton Vernis leather baby pack; in

Christian Lacroix Couture, 2002

2000 the Louis Vuitton "graffiti" pochette reigned; and in 2001 the Sonia Rykiel Domino, the John Galliano Trailer for Dior, the Hermès Birkin, and the Balenciaga Saddle all beckoned like sirens. In such a hothouse atmosphere of fierce competition, bags are bred like freakish hybrids. Sprouting handles made of buffalo horn or combat straps and bodies of chunky turquoise, chicken feathers, or beaten bronze, this year's "It" bags are *jolie laide*. Designed to jolt a jaded palette, they revel in incongruity, brash shapes, and bold contrasts. Fendi's

*Stella McCartney,*
*soft-rock style, 2002*

Ostrik bag was
inspired by an oyster and
Sonia Rykiel's black leather ruffle
bag looks like a creature from the deep.
In the quest for "It" the handbag has
become almost physically aggressive: a
long Gaultier clutch that looks a bit like
a night stick, a Moschino evening bag in
military canvas. Perhaps the uncertainty
of a new century compels women to literally
get a grip onto fashion's strongest symbol of
security—the handbag.

# ACKNOWLEDGMENTS

**S**ally Wofford Girand, my agent, brought the team together for *Handbags* and deserves a nice big thank you. Eri Morita carries the visual weight of this project, she shot hundreds of handbags for this book with untiring originality. I thank her for her visual intelligence, innate styling, and precision. My brilliant editor, Ruth Sullivan, believed in bags from the beginning and brought this book to fruition with a will of iron. Her instincts for a great bag or bad sentence taught me a great deal and forged a rich vision. Thanks to Janet Vicario for a fresh and truly scrumptious design effort and to Natsumi Uda for creating order out of chaos; to Leora Kahn for sleuthing out the best bag collections in the world; to Jessica Firger for her inspired research; to Aaron Clendening for being "so fashion"; to Joni Miller for a gazillion clippings and good quotes; to Elizabeth Gaynor for color genius; to Peter Workman for a great work space; to the Workman publicity and marketing departments for their inspired ideas; and to Mr. and Mrs. Frank Greally for their long hours.

The following people also made special contributions to *Handbags:* Katherine Adzima, Jessica Adams, Kelli Bagley, Donna May Bolinger, Robin Bowden, Patty Bozza, Melinda Brown, Sharon Crawford, Mimi Crume, Matteo de Cosmo, Denise DeLuca, Anita Dickhuth, Amanda Ducker, Wendy Frost, Massimo Giannoni, Richard Goodwin, Helga Groves, Karen Handley, Bruce Harris,

Peter Hermann, Emilia Hernandez, Marta Jaremko, Michael, Margot and Matthew Johnson, Ken Klemann, Elisabetta Lachi, Francesca Leoni, Samantha Lang, Karen Larkin, Leila Listo, Karen Markham, Nancy Mizrahi, Barney McAll, Amy Marth, Barbara Mateer, Moses Said Nassar, Karlo Pastrovic, Alicia Richardson, Erin Roberts, David Roby, Marina Rosenbaum, Alice Sykes, Helene and Francois Valentine, Nancy Walsh, Lisa Wells, Desire Brand Management, Dennis Wong, and Di Yee.

Much respect to the collectors who generously lent their bags to this project: Janice Berkson at Deco Jewels, Rita Brookoff at Legacy, Elisa Casas at LaPochette.com, Francine Cohen, Mary Efron of Mary Efron Antiques, Joy Liotta of GIOIA design, Anthony Luciano, Ross and Irene Langlands of Nomadic Rug Traders, Sydney, Kim Hastreiter, Cesar Padilla at Cherry Resource, Jill Stuart, Mark Walsh and Leslie Chin, Laura Wills of Screaming Mimi's.

A special appreciation for the knowledge and patience of the following curators, designers, and design history experts: Barbara and Henry Bolan, Dilys Blum, Oriole Cullen, Stephanie Day Iverson, Isabelle Jamin and Benoit Puech, Jill Davison at *Harper's Bazaar,* Cecile de la Perraudiere and Xavier Dixsaut at Louis Vuitton, Menehould Du Chapelle at Hermès, Fred Dennis, Silvia Venturini Fendi, Simon Doonan, George Epaminondas, Carlos Falchi, Rosella Giardini at Moschino, Pamela Golbin, Robert Gottleib, Lulu Guinness, Titi Halle, Will Hardy, Marion Hume, Luigi Limberti, Judith Lieber, Doctor Rosita Neno, Angela Paoli at Fendi, Soizic Pfaff at Christian Dior, Stefania Ricci, Sonia Rykiel, Valerie Steele, John Truex and Richard Lambertson, Mayumi Yoshizawa.

Thanks to the following institutions for their generosity and resources: The Bonnie Cashin Archive, The Chanel Archive, The Museum of Fine Arts Boston, The Detroit Institute of Art, The Deutsch Leder Museum, The Christian Dior Archive, William Doyle Galleries, Cora Ginsberg Fine Arts LLC, The Museum at the Fashion Institute of Technology, The Emile Hermès Collection, The Metropolitan Museum of Art, The Museum of London, Le Musée de l'Art et Textile de la Mode, The National Museum of the American Indian, The Philadelphia Museum of Fine Arts, Museo Salvatore Ferragamo, The Victoria and Albert Museum, The Wolfsonian, and The Smithsonian Institute.

A few bags in this book came into our hands without a label or any trace of the original maker, so my thanks go to every invisible artisan behind a label, and to the centuries of women who have loved and cherished the handbag.

*Jamin Puech,
Carioca bag,
2002*

# Photo Credits

## ABOUT THE AUTHOR

Stuart Conway

Anna Johnson was given a sequined art deco evening bag at the age of five and used it for carrying crayons; in high school she had her school satchel custom embroidered; and in her years as a freelance writer she tried everything from a raffia basket to a Balinese backpack. Working as a journalist for *Elle, Vanity Fair, Vogue* (UK and Australia), *Vogue Entertaining, Marie Claire Lifestyle, Condé Nast Traveler,* and *MSN Women,* and dabbling in illustration, TV presenting, and home sewing helped refine her taste, but intensified the quest for the perfect handbag. She is the author of *Three Black Skirts: All You Need to Survive.* Currently at work on a novel, Anna lives in Chinatown in New York City, but never buys designer fakes.